The Press and Main Street

The Press and Main Street

El País—Journalism in Democratic Spain

Juan Luis Cebrián

Translated by Brian Nienhaus

Ann Arbor
THE UNIVERSITY OF MICHIGAN PRESS

Library of Congress Cataloging-in-Publication Data

Cebrián, Juan Luis, 1945–
    [Prensa y la calle. English]
    The press and Main Street : El País—journalism in democratic
Spain / Juan Luis Cebrián ; translated by Brian Nienhaus.
        p.   cm.
    Translation of: La prensa y la calle.
    Includes bibliographical references.
    ISBN 0-472-10115-3 (alk. paper) :
    1. Journalism—Spain—History—20th century.   2. País (Madrid,
Spain : 1976)   I. Title.
PN5314.C413   1989
076'.1—dc20   89-27000
                                                                              CIP

Illustrations courtesy of *El País*.

Foreword

When Juan Luis Cebrián shuffled into my office at the University of Michigan, I thought he was a new graduate student looking for the School of Social Work offices down the hall.

Part of this was my problem: I had spent years working with European editors-in-chief. Their tailoring had always shamed me. Their air of infallible authority, combined with a somehow sinister suggestion of connections leading directly from their desks to schoolboy chums now at THE VERY TOP, never failed to unnerve me. No American counterpart I had met at *Time*, the *New York Times* or the *Washington Post* could possibly measure up.

But here slouched Cebrián, fuzzy brown-purple tweeds of undistinguished origin sliding from unprepossessing shoulders in ways that fairly shouted "I do *not* cut quite a figure!" That, it turned out, was the point.

There is no *bella figura* in Juan Luis Cebrián. Nor was there inherited money or fancy family connections. Somehow, he managed to climb the slippery ladder of Franco-era

Spanish journalism without getting his hands slimey. He reported as much as he could, when and for whom he could. When forced to compromise more than he wanted, he quit. In 1974 he detected what he sardonically calls "our forty years of peace" about to end with the Generalissimo's hold on life. This proved to be a trigger of fundamental and totally unexpected magnitude. Although he had not realized it, Cebrián's career as reporter and editor had been merely the caterpillar and pupa stages of vocational metamorphosis. Franco's last illness hatched Cebrián into entrepreneur-publisher, a winged creature bent on creating a new kind of newspaper.

El País ("The Nation") would have the format of France's *le Monde*, the tone of the *Manchester Guardian*, the reliability of the *Frankfurter Allgemeine Zeitung*, and the independence of the *Washington Post*. Its initial funding, however, would in no way resemble any of the agglomerations of capital those models represent. Cebrián's road to editorial independence led through small investors, none of whom contributed more than a few thousand dollars.

In our last meeting, he retained the remarkable air first detected in Ann Arbor. He projects incorruptibility because what really interests him in life is unrelated to money.

Oddly, that stance probably explains the phenomenal financial success of *El País*. Spain had slipped into near-total journalistic corruption. The new paper's independence of money attracted it irresistibly. Within its first decade of existence, *El País* was the country's biggest advertising vehicle. But there is nothing surprising about the editorial triumphs. Integrity was the "marketing strategy" that has attracted 350,000 daily and 900,000 Sunday readers, nearly twice as many as its largest Madrid rival. Integrity also explains the common understanding that if the coming of democracy in Spain was a precondition for *El País's* creation, the reverse is equally true. Without *El País,* Spanish democracy would not long endure.

Cebrián's influence is not confined to Spain. He merely managed to create a new world model there, in the birthplace of inquisitorial intolerance and cradle of the world's longest-run Fascism. His retooling of American-style journalism is widely admired in Europe. In France, a daily with a radical pedigree inherited from Jean-Paul Sartre and Mao Tse-tung now rivals *le Monde* in influence if not yet in circulation. Not bad for the second incarnation of *Liberation,* dating from 1978. Britain has the *Independent,* of more conventional origins and even more recent birth. They amplify the *El País* message: Vibrant, independent, substantial journalism can outsell the alternatives, even in an era dominated by the Hersants and Murdochs, not to mention the Harte-Hankses and Gannetts.

Which brings us to the U.S. newspapers today, *USA Today,* and how far Cebrián's experiment is from anything in the United States, from which he drew fundamental inspiration. In significant ways, the American newspaper industry resembles Bugs Bunny at the moment he looks down after bounding off the cliff. For years, newspapers managed not to do that even though television had surpassed them as the primary news medium by the mid-1960s and total readership (62 million) has not risen appreciably for thirty years despite an explosion in the number of households. The momentum of surging cash flow kept newspapers looking up when the solid ground was running out.

No longer. In 1988, profits fell sharply, putting total return on investment for newspapers in unfamiliar and unwelcome company relative to other U.S. industrial sectors. Newspapers need rebirth so badly that discomfort replaced bonhomie at the twin conventions that drum the annual tom-toms of newspaper journalism. The money people of the American Newspaper Publishers Association (ANPA) met in Chicago. For the first time in memory, an entire morning was devoted to circulation and readership. The product people of the American Society of Newspaper Editors (ASNE) circled the wagons in Washington. Their key event: a panel debate on "Who's a Journalist?" featuring leading newspaper people and TV talk-show hosts ranging from the occasionally sublime (Donahue) to the frequently ridiculous (Morton Downey, Jr.).

The newspaper people tried to dissociate themselves and journalism from the television hosts, whose on-camera fist-fight (Geraldo Rivera) and advice to guests—"Suck my armpit!" (Downey)—were shown to the largest working-session audience in ASNE history. But the distancing failed. Many even admitted feeling more than a little uncomfortable when Donahue, the most sedate broadcaster, fixed a cool blue eye on Jack Nelson of the *Los Angeles Times* and asked why the newspaperman thought it so important to decide who's a journalist and who isn't.

Before Nelson finished his explanation, Downey broke in to shout "You're not a journalist. You're a snob!" The charge was pure rubbish. Nelson most certainly *is* a true-blue journalist: one of the best, at that. And he is no stuffed shirt. But Donahue's query and Downey's outrage went right to the heart of the identity crisis in American newspaper journalism. The industry is so bent on sounding statesmanlike while pandering to shareholder financial demands that it hasn't been able to keep in touch with certain realities— like what expands audiences.

For newspapers not less than other retailing operations, young adults eighteen to twenty-nine are the make/break market because they represent future sales. Newspapers are losing readers of that key age. In 1967, 60 percent read a newspaper every day. By last year, that figure had been cut by more than half; a bare 29 percent of "the yuppie generation" bother to read the local newspaper. But for comparative purposes, it is more useful to switch the focus from the failures of American newspapering to its one truly new departure.

USA Today is a genuine invention. The distinction from "improved standard model" is necessary to set it apart from papers such as the *Philadelphia Inquirer,* which under Gene Roberts's leadership and Knight-Ridder ownership rose from sleazy second to national prominence as the pound-for-pound best newspaper in the country. *USA Today* cannot be considered best of anything, nor the worst, for that matter, because it is the *only* one of its kind: a general-readership publication in daily newspaper format designed specifically to tap the pool of national advertising money that floats television and magazines.

Opinions differ about *USA Today's* profitability. For present purposes, that matters far less than recognizing how different in concept and mission it is from *El País* and its spiritual cousins in Europe. It doesn't take long to get the message about Allen Neuharth, the hardscrabble kid from Pumpkin Center, South Dakota, who built Gannett into a money machine which then poured coin into *USA Today*, his personal brainchild and monument. Neuharth is famous for ducal trappings, beginning with his palace in Cocoa Beach. It has a staircase that raises like a drawbridge. The outfits are expensive and blackjack flashy. The Gannett jet, famous for in-flight three-star seafood with Neuharth aboard, made direct connections with the limousine. When holding corporate court, Neuharth matched vassal executives' seats with the message he would give them. To the world at large, the gaze said, among other things, "Beware. I am *connected.*"

In short, at the top of the journalistic corporate heap in America sits our only innovator (or maybe sat; Neuharth recently retired), and his dreams are full of money. In the essays herein, one of them written specifically for Americans, a fabulously successful Spanish publisher argues that money is important, but it is equally important to prevent it from being primary.

This is a moment of considerable malaise and even some fear among American editors and publishers. They would do well to consider an alternative to the money culture journalism of their country, as represented by a midwesterner who bears an uncanny resemblance to traditional European editorial chieftains. I recommend they listen to a rumpled fellow who comes from a place where they tilt at windmills, true enough. But the lance in his hand has rescued the best in journalism in ways *USA Today* was not designed to do, and made it pay handsomely.

Charles R. Eisendrath
Ann Arbor, 1989

Translator's Note

In a traditional translator's task, I have added footnotes to explain names and events presumably unfamiliar to English-speaking readers. One usually does this after completing the translation itself, and when I began to do so I was struck by how much of this book needed no explanation. It is filled with a rhetoric of democracy, of freedom of expression and service to the reader. My prose weaknesses apart, it reads familiarly because many of its ideas are our own.

As it became clear that the years of Spanish dictator Francisco Franco were drawing to a close, a number of intellectuals and journalists, among them Juan Luis Cebrián, made plans for a newspaper that would adequately serve the coming democracy. In retrospect it makes sense that they would turn to the Anglo-American literature on the subject. They read and admired our tradition, sought our motivating ideas, and put them into practice.

The Spanish, however, were compelled to apply these quite old ideas in the second half of the twentieth century.

Their efforts gave them new substance and life. So in a sense the footnotes I have added could mislead the reader: They flag the obviously strange names and events, but they do not indicate the areas in the text where an old idea has been given new inflection in journalistic practice. The most consequential ideas, the most revealing differences between this Spanish vision of a democratic press and our own, may well pass by the reader unnoticed precisely because they come wrapped in the familiar language.

The experience of *El País* suggests that substantial differences exist. This recent innovation in national journalism is powerfully informing and variously entertaining. And when it informs it can be heavy. It would not hurt, for example, to have a textbook or two around when reading its business or labor pages. Politicians across the ideological spectrum fight to get not only their names or faces but their ideas into its pages. Many of the world's great thinkers and writers regularly appear in the paper, whether or not they are trained in the production of clear journalistic prose. Three years after its appearance in 1976 it was regarded as Spain's paper of record (see table 1). Yet there are indications that *El País* is not merely the *New York Times* of Spain.

El País is also a popular paper. It is the largest circulating daily in Spain, and it continues to receive hundreds of thousands of letters to the editor from all walks of Spanish life. Over the years it has become a source of substantial and reliable income for its parent firm, Promotora de Informaciones, S.A. (PRISA), with healthy income growth from both newsstand sales *and* advertising.

Evidently our own national innovations in daily journal-

TABLE 1. Average Daily and Sunday Circulation of Major Spanish Daily Newspapers, 1975–87, in Thousands

Years	El País		La Vanguardia		ABC		Diario 16		El Periódico		Ya	
1975–76	—	—	220	287	186	398	—	—	—	—	168	253
1976–77	129	144	206	273	157	341	—	—	—	—	140	221
1977–78	128	181	196	266	136	290	59	—	—	—	124	198
1978–79	146	203	186	255	124	269	47	—	53	—	122	199
1979–80	184	263	188	268	131	290	51	—	72	—	118	195
1980–81	234	357	193	281	136	300	84	—	99	—	112	184
1982	296	471	196	303	127	283	125	—	112	155	110	169
1982–83	340	553	192	303	146	302	130	—	127	160	105	159
1984	347	583	194	308	157	300	128	180	128	161	96	145
1985	348	613	191	N.A.	219	342	130	192	137	184	88	132
1986	360	682	195	313	235	405	135	193	151	235	80	112
1987	373	758	195	316	247	415	137	183	154	246	75	104

Source: Composite statistics from the August 8, 1986, and July 31, 1988, issues of El País, from data obtained from the Spanish Office of Circulation Auditing.

Note: Yearly breakdowns not evenly distributed. For each newspaper the first figure cited is for daily circulation and the second for Sunday circulation.

ism are informed by the notion that to receive popular approval a newspaper must be a highly colorful object cast in minimalist prose. The paper that best embodies this caricature continues to demonstrate uncertain profit potential. With the example of *El País* in mind, our innovations seem puzzling. I wonder how long our print journalism will see its task as one of mimicking a medium it cannot hope to succeed against, and how long it will be before even the business-minded among us remember that in some instances it makes sense not to mimic, but to differentiate one's product in order to succeed in the marketplace. If and when such thoughts make their presence felt in our journalistic world, I believe it will also be easier for us to see those subtle changes in meaning and emphasis Mr. Cebrián and his generation of journalists have given to our ideas.

For those who do not see our situation in this way there remains much of value in this book. It is the chronicle of a very important time in contemporary Spain, and its author has become a classic example of a great person. By all accounts Mr. Cebrián is regarded as one of the most powerful and influential people in the country. It must be noted that he left the top editorial position at *El País* in 1988 for a higher executive position in PRISA, and in doing so may have taken a half step away from the inner circles of effective power. Still, in Juan Luis Cebrián the future biographer will discover a journalistic prodigy and personable genius. By age thirty-one, when he became editor in chief of *El País,* he had already accumulated thirteen years of journalistic experience, many of them at senior editorial levels, including a period as news director for the first channel of Spanish National Television. The intensity of his journalistic and editorial experience is perhaps unique, and these essays contain a great deal of what will ultimately be attributable to his particular vision and style. To imagine this vision and capture this style was my most formidable challenge; it is certainly where the discriminating reader will find I have taken the greatest leaps away from literal lexical and syntactical translation.

I am, of course, responsible for any errors in translation and footnotes, and also for the orientation suggested in this note. A number of people went out of their way to enable me to complete this project. The bulk of it was translated with support from the Marsh Fund for Journalism Research at the Department of Communication, the University of Michigan. The person most supportive from the outset has been Professor Charles Eisendrath, director of the Journalist in Residence Program at the University of Michigan. Professor Eisendrath was also responsible for bringing Mr. Cebrián to Michigan as a visiting professor in the fall of 1986. It was of no small relief to me to find that the person whose work I had toiled over for many months was a genuinely warm and decent human being. As a result of this visit the English edition has two chapters (9 and 10) and a preface not found in the Spanish original. To help translate this new material I thank Ms. Isabel Bustamante. For the visual materials, including the *Máximo* cartoons with which we have begun each chapter (and whose meaning we do not explain, since in many instances we cannot) I thank *El País*. Robert Dickerson, Jr., is to be thanked for innumerable instances of help and advice along the way, as are, finally, the members of Harry's House in Ann Arbor, Michigan. On that score I find it wise to recommend that one not undertake a book translation while teaching and pursuing a doctoral degree, unless they feel they have to, and only then if they have support in what passes for home life during such busy times, as I had at Harry's.

Brian Nienhaus
Ann Arbor, Michigan
March, 1988

Preface to the U.S. Edition

It has been more than eight years now since this book was published in Madrid by Nuestra Cultura in October of 1980, yet I am surprised at the currency of the issues and events it contains, and at the degree to which I still hold to the opinions developed there. My publisher in the United States has very appropriately asked that I update some of the facts and clarify certain expressions foreign to the U.S. readership. Well, this very necessary task has been quick to carry out all the same, since the essential themes of the book still hold true. I am referring not only to its deeper analyses or to its motivating ideology, but also to the concrete issues whose relevance should still render them objects of our concern and not monstrosities from which to avert one's gaze. Looking carefully at the Spanish press now, only one substantial change has taken place since the original publication of this book: the liquidation of the Movement newspaper chain, an institutional leftover from the Franco regime that had remained in government hands until the socialists decided to privatize it in 1983–84. Paradoxically, it turns out, the realization of this goal (elaborated in my book in a couple of places) occurred at the hand of a leftist government. During its tenure as leader of parliamentary opposition, the PSOE[1] was a strong proponent of a policy of maintaining a state press in some institutional form. Its party theoreticians believed that such a conglomerate would serve to balance the shift to the right which, in their opinion, was taking place within the "bourgeois" press. Once in power, however, the socialists hurried to rid themselves of the papers, since they had been so closely identified with Franco's old propaganda machine. Each of those newspapers had a solidly entrenched group of old regime journalists on their staffs, and that one fact was sufficient to render any effort to democratize them impossible. But beyond this, the breakup of the Movement press can be seen as an instance of a much broader policy of privatization taking place in many other sectors of the economy.[2]

The sale of government newspapers was carried out in reasonably honest fashion. On only one occasion (that of *El Sur* of Málaga), did journalists and workers attend an auction of newspaper assets and, with generous public assistance, take ownership of a paper and form a cooperative.

---

1. Spanish Socialist Workers Party.—TRANS.

2. Why did the PSOE, a socialist party, adopt a policy of privatization in 1982? To a large degree the public industrial sector under Franco had become a repository of the mistakes and special interests of people close to him. The socialists felt that moving these entities out of the protective sphere of the state would force them to adopt more rational business and accounting routines. The PSOE received strong support in the 1982 elections from younger and more highly educated segments of the population who saw in the party a way to infuse the corporate environment with some meritocratic energies.—TRANS.

The rest of the newspapers (which numbered more than twenty at that time) were sold to private firms. Some of them—the papers in Santander and Jaén, for example—received indirect support from the PSOE. But overall, the decision to liquidate this newspaper chain has done much to clarify the structure of the Spanish press system.

We cannot report any analogous movement toward clarity in the case of Spanish television. Although I originally argued in this book that the public proprietary character of television was not an essential issue, time and TVE's[3] performance under the socialist government have made me change my mind.

The constant manipulation of television by political power in Spain has given more than sufficient reason for the demand for a law to establish private television. Now this long-awaited law has finally been passed by Spanish Parliament. But it has been so gutted by socialist government interests that its very existence is deceiving. The law has defrauded the hopes and expectations its passage had originally inspired.

Beyond the maze of cautions and interventionist conditions contained in the law, one clear motivation seems to emerge: through it the government now intends to control not just public television but private television as well.

The other journalistic issues explored in this book are still current. Neither professional secrecy nor the conscience clause[4] have received sufficient statutory definition, and

---

3. Spanish National Television.—TRANS.
4. Professional secrecy and the conscience clause are discussed more fully in chapter 8.—TRANS.

there are numerous new cases to add to those already mentioned in this book. The courts regularly hear cases brought by journalists seeking protection of their sources under the constitution, but to date the accumulating legal opinions have not done much to clarify the matter, and the status of the conscience clause is even less clear. Although pressure to pass a new comprehensive press law has decreased and the status of the Law of the Press of 1966[5] has become increasingly nebulous (the law has effectively fallen into disuse), furor over the administration and deteriorating performance of our schools of journalism is a clear reality. In fact, the situation worsened with the opening of the College of Journalism in Catalonia. The authority for its establishment has been appealed to the constitutional Court by the public prosecutor. More importantly, the whole legal status of the Spanish press has worsened with the passage of new laws against terrorism and for the protection of personal honor. These laws constitute serious threats to the exercise of freedom of the press.

Finally, I would like to mention that the last two chapters

---

5. In the mid-1960s Franco's Information and Tourism minister Manuel Fraga Ibarne helped develop a package of statutory decrees governing the press that were, in effect, less strict than those previously on the books. The package was entitled the Law of the Press of 1966, but it was and is more commonly referred to as the "Fraga Law." Fraga himself is often mentioned in the pages that follow, and for good reason. He has been one of the most important political figures in Spain for the last quarter century. He held various ministerial posts under Franco, most notably that of tourism during the economic boom years of the 1960s. During that time he was considered a liberal Francoist. During the transition to democracy in the 1970s, he decided to remain apart from the center coalition that won the first elections. He formed his own right-of-center party, the Popular Alliance (AP), which since the collapse of the center coalition has become the leading party of parliamentary opposition. He is an incredibly prolific writer and a man of considerable intellect.—TRANS.

of the present book, "Journalists and Politicians" and "Across the Water," were not part of the original edition. The latter was written specifically for the U.S. edition. With these small corrections now in place, I should say that the panorama this work explores remains virtually the same as it appeared six years ago. Indeed, the lack of meaningful progress toward better mass communication should lead us all to do some serious thinking. After the aborted coup of 1981[6] and the ensuing socialist electoral victory in 1982, Spanish democracy seems to have entered into a period of normalization, which has frequently been confused with stagnation. The existence of a strong and independent press continues to be the principal guarantee that democracy will not perish, though now not from a coup but from an accumulation of self-satisfaction.

Juan Luis Cebrián
Madrid, Spain

---

6. This coup attempt is discussed in footnote 2 in chapter 9.—TRANS.

Preface to the Spanish Edition

An Expression of Solidarity

The disgraceful fact that journalists and newspapers have themselves become protagonists in the news they report should perhaps suffice as an initial justification for the appearance of this slim volume. Its publisher, Nuestra Cultura, has become the subject of malevolent legal actions that today loom as a threat to the freedom of expression, actions which in this specific instance have resulted in the seizure of *The Little Red Schoolbook*.[1] I am not about to take part in the theoretical discussions concerning that little manual; it has already received more ink than it deserves in the Western press. Rather, I feel it more important to point out

---

1. Published in Spain as *El libro rojo del cole*. The original book, by Soren Hansen and Jesper Jenson, was translated into English and published in New York in 1971 by Basic Books. The publisher of the Spanish translation no longer exists.—TRANS.

that there have always and everywhere been inquisitors who come up with social, legal, political, moral, ethical, convenient, and creative justifications for the unjustifiable barbarity of book burning. Thus it is no accident that through this particular publisher this personal and arbitrary compilation of some of my thoughts on journalism now appears. The defense of freedom is attained through the solidarity of men. And in the face of such repressive acts as these, the lack of intellectual solidarity in this country merits more than commentary.

I have little or perhaps nothing to say about the book itself. It contains conference papers, articles and essays written on diverse journalistic themes over the last five years. It is not a scientific monograph or a formal treatment of the problems of written communication, but rather a sampling from my experience with—and reflections on—a particular subject. And in the last analysis, it is a subject that can never receive too much attention.

Undoubtedly, many and important ideas that are related to the topics outlined in the contents will remain briefly mentioned or insufficiently developed and some completely ignored. But the book as a whole stands as representative of my thoughts—now there's a pretentious phrase!—on some basic journalistic questions, and as such should prove of use to journalistic scholars and to those who are simply curious.

Some of the material here has also been published in specialized and limited-circulation journals. "Journalism as a Profession" and "The Impact of Image" were commissioned by the March Foundation, and "Freedom of the Press in the Constitution" was written for a seminar sponsored by the

Human Sciences Foundation. Some of the articles were previously unpublished, and of these, a few were delivered at conferences.

Finally, I would like to make clear that in these pages I do not pretend to support or develop any particular doctrine or school of thought. I have always been a journalist and have prided myself on being only that. Which is to say, I suppose, that I share some of those peculiar and questionable qualities that mark those who practice this nocturnal and somewhat maligned trade, one that neither television nor the world of computers appears to be able to do away with. In short, I am internally compelled to resist the traps of scholarly classification and praise from the prestigious, and will not allow myself to become pigeonholed as another contributor to the pedagogical literature on journalism. This book, then, contains quite a bit of passion and not a little brusqueness, but I have tried throughout to be honest, and the results are, at least, sincere. And if it proves useful to someone in some way, then praise be to God in all His Holy Glory.

Juan Luis Cebrián
Madrid, Spain
July 1980

Contents

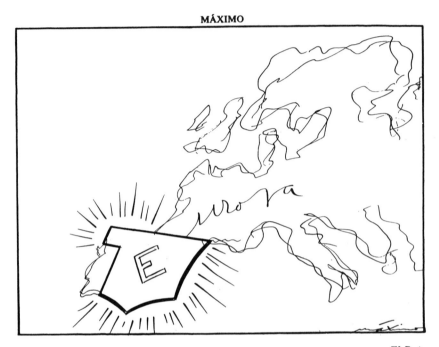

El País

Chapter 1

The Press in Democratic Spain

One of the common characteristics of *dictatorships*—whether of the right or the left, with *authoritarian* being their sweetest euphemistic label—is the direct control they wield over their spheres of information and culture. This control is maintained not only through censorship, seizures, and persecution, but also through direct structural and administrative controls. Logically, the more absolutely a dictatorship exercises its power, the more restrictive and effective it is in these spheres.

Not all authoritarian regimes are equal in the degree of threat they pose to freedom. Nor for that matter, in spite of their formal similarity, do the democracies show equal potential for political and cultural development in their countries. Thus from a combination of international cynicism and objective political necessity, the world allows oligarchies firmly maintained in power by violence to be labeled democratic. And one can also find a variety of authoritarian regimes that occasionally offer degrees of flexibility in the freedom of expression rivaling those of the so-called phantom democracies.

Authoritarian regimes have a set of philosophical postulates to guide them in their maintenance of power. These ideas will normally reflect and determine the ways in which they repress the freedom of thought and the flow of news. The existence of a tangible, official truth in the possession of a group holding the reins of power requires its simultaneous propagation and defense from "conspiratorial" or "erroneous" attacks. This holds true for both capitalist and socialist dictatorships, for systems of party dictatorship and for family oligarchies ruling tiny tinhorn republics. But the hostile attitude of public powers toward the mass media is not due solely to the former's ideological architecture or practices. Even in democracies of proven tradition, governments and the other social institutions strive to control the press and other channels of communication. Although this behavior goes against the postulates of freedom that these same regimes say they defend, it does correspond well to the habits and requirements of power.

For its part, a free press contributes to the diffusion of that power. The press in a modern democracy does not just produce information. It plays an analytical and critical role: it checks and disputes. It is a source of power itself, and has come to be called the fourth estate. It refuses to be routinely subjected to the conditioning and stereotypical schemes of the "establishment." Well, at least not all of the press falls in line. This journalistic independence, this quality of acquired power that some communications entities achieve explains why governments want to control them. If newspapers actually carry out this adversarial function, they then threaten the operations of those in government.

But in a democracy the systematic criticism of power does not necessarily lead to an erosion of power itself. It can actually be a quite useful gauge of the acceptability of a regime's ideology. A truly democratic government, one really in touch with its people, will always be able to take advantage of the information gained from the criticism and adverse opinions leveled at it. There is the traditional notion here that a politician should learn to eat his daily crow at breakfast. But this most worthy tradition seems to be losing popularity among the Western ruling class, probably because they are nicely disposed of too many shotguns with which to kill crows whenever they want. They do not realize, or if they do, they are just not concerned, that every time one of these birds gets bumped off something of democratic essence dies, too.

Perhaps all these things explain why in Spain the democratic powers have not yet seen fit to guarantee a logically functioning free press in any structural fashion. This has already forced many organs of public opinion to close down, unable to sustain heavy economic losses. Some of them, paradoxically—as in the case of *Cuadernos para el Diálogo*[1]—

---

1. *Cuadernos para el Diálogo*, literally "Notebooks for Dialogue," was founded in 1963 by the liberal Catholic Joaquín Ruiz Giménez, ex-ambassador to Rome and minister of education under Franco. Caught up in the spirit of the Second Vatican Council, he founded this publication to promote Vatican ideals inside Spain. Presumably because of his church ties, his publication was somewhat immune from censorship and harassment. He remained in the government until 1964, trying to modify Francoism from within, but the task was too large. One commentator likened his efforts to those of "a sister of charity preaching chastity in a whorehouse" (Paul Preston, *The Triumph of Democracy in Spain* [London: Methuen, 1986], 82). Ruiz Giménez subsequently passed into the moderate opposition. Cebrián at age twenty was one of the original members of the editorial staff at *Cuadernos*. See David Gilmour, *The Transformation of Spain: From Franco to the Constitutional Monarchy* (New York: Quartet Books, 1985) and Preston 1986.—Trans.

played key roles under very adverse circumstances in the long struggle against dictatorship and for democratic pluralism. *Cuadernos* was without a doubt the first liberating effort of a classically oppositional nature to exist in the world of public opinion under Franco. Many democratic leaders were given their first forum in its pages. Today a large number of them are representatives in parliament, and for them that magazine was the symbol and substance of an authentic citizens' movement against the repression of the old regime. Nevertheless, it died of the same disease that has killed many other newspapers and magazines: negligible reading habits among the Spanish people, and economic anomalies created by the previous regime's mistreatment of the sector, undoubtedly because they did not hold it in high regard. Right now a Law for State Support of the Press,[2] with all its problems and opportunities for political manipulation and pressure, has been presented for public debate. But an independent Spanish press—a sector in profound crisis—does not need a subsidy law to survive, it needs legislation that will remove some very real obstacles. State protection of the newsprint monopolies, the continued existence of the old official newspaper chain of the Franco regime, national television's cornering of the advertising market, and most certainly the lack of an efficient distribution infrastructure, are all conditions that afflict the media sector and threaten to stifle independent voices in the press. Part of the current problem, of course,

---

2. This was legislation to supersede the Law of the Press of 1966, or the "Fraga Law." As mentioned in the U.S. Preface, it was not passed and Spain is still without a post-Franco press law.—TRANS.

was caused by the proliferation of publications during the first months of the democracy, many of which had not properly evaluated the narrowness of the Spanish reader market. Hence, the panorama of the mass media in Spain today is tremendously confusing. On the one hand, an economic crisis mortally threatens a number of publications. On the other, there does not yet exist any clarification of the legal status of the press. This immense juridical uncertainty remains even though the constitution has consecrated such progressive journalistic concepts as the conscience clause and the right to professional secrecy.[3] Television and radio await their statutes, while the old propaganda apparatus of the dictatorship remains intact.[4] The administration, meanwhile, has not abandoned the old persecutorial tactics. Government lawsuits against journalists and newspapers have mushroomed.

Democracy, for which the Spanish press worked so long and under such hostile conditions, has not treated journalists very well. The negative attitudes of the present political class toward the press are comparable to—and sometimes worse than—those of the previous regime's leaders. While it is true that actual circumstances do not permit today's leaders the same range of reactions the previous government had, and also that this range of possibilities is supposedly limited by their own convictions, one can indeed detect that same intolerance, which comes from those con-

---

3. These issues are discussed in detail in chapter 8.—TRANS.
4. Cebrián refers to the Movement newspaper chain, which, as he noted in the Preface to the U.S. Edition, was dismantled and privatized by the current socialist government of Spain under Felipe González.—TRANS.

ditions and motives noted at the beginning of this chapter. In nineteenth century Spain, Mariano José de Larra[5] ventured that "to write in Spain is to weep." He ended up committing suicide while the nation around him convulsed in political wranglings. When he saw that his liberal friends, once in power, were neither better nor more liberal than those who had preceded them, he was struck with disillusionment. Now it would be unjust not to recognize that in today's Spain we have advanced considerably: there is really no reason for a Spanish journalist to shoot himself these days. Nevertheless, a certain Larranesque disillusionment is invading professional circles as they witness the installation of a new political apparatus that is incorporating the vices of the old. To shrink away from an investigation of the importance of this phenomenon is tantamount to acquiescing in the beginning of the destruction of our new democratic regime. If it is truly not our lot to commit suicide, then we might well join our voices with Larra and cry "God help us."

---

5. Mariano José de Larra (1809–37) is arguably the greatest figure in the history of Spanish journalism. Writing during a time when romanticism had begun to make its presence felt in Madrid, his journalistic articles were often masterpieces in the use of literary forms to deliver sharp commentaries on social and political life. His method stems in part from the exigencies of getting ideas past the censors—the object of attack may be denied if given in indirect form—but often that same indirectness gives much more impact to the commentary, perhaps because it assumes that the reader can and will make the necessary reconstructions of meaning and intention. In any case, I can think of no figure comparable to Larra in U.S. journalistic history. Larra shot himself to death in 1837 moments after his mistress announced to him that their affair was at an end.—TRANS.

El País

Chapter 2

The Impact of Image

All too often in the social sciences and in communication studies, research is carried out by amateurs, and I fear that my efforts here may be yet another example of this phenomenon. We journalists are narrators of news, not experts in the fields of semiology, linguistics, social psychology or sociology, areas through which one may construct theoretical analyses of the effects of mass communication. Although confession like this is certainly in order before proceeding any further, I do consider myself an attentive and interested follower of the media, and an avid reader of whatever is produced on the subject. And if I can bring into this discussion something from my eighteen years of experience as a radio and print journalist, it may well be of help in illuminating certain areas where the professional theoreticians seem to wander in the dark. In effect, those who are commonly called *communication scientists* in our country often do not know the actual conditions and practices of the mass media, or the human side of those who work in them. They seek to cover their ignorance under a blanket of pedantry, obscuring things that were long clear to everyone else.

Fortunately, the theme of this chapter is worded so ambiguously that we can get on with the discussion confident that the venture will not be boring: we have the latitude to discuss what we wish.

Traditionally, or at least generally and in an unconscious way, the word is considered the fundamental unit of expression for the print and electronic media. Assiduously ignored are the eminent roles played by photographs and illustrations, and the fact that some newspapers and magazines expressly seek their fortune by presenting their messages graphically. Also overlooked is the symbol-image power of words themselves. Finally, it tends to be forgotten that a newspaper itself, in its entirety, is a symbolic object: it is not just read line by line but is seen as a whole, and if that were not enough, touched.

This conceptualization of a newspaper as a visual object and of words as graphic designs will occupy our attention for some time to follow. But before that, I would like to digress for a moment to take up this tactile aspect of newspapers and magazines. The sense of touch is the least sophisticated and intellectual of those known, even less so than those of smell or taste. Albert Kienz[1] has argued that messages can be defined in terms of the sensory media employed by their receivers. But it is only the visual and auditory senses that have been studied in depth. Nevertheless—

---

1. Albert Kienz, *Pour analyser les media, l'analyse de contenu* (Paris: Mame, 1971), 23.

though perhaps secondarily—newspapers are made to be touched. The quality of the paper and—especially in less evolved or less literate communities—the format are essential considerations in the process of putting a publication on the market. Quite significant in Spain is the rejection of the broadsheet newspaper, which dates from *ABC*'s[2] pioneering switch to a tabloid format. The reader still believes that, independent of content, newspapers in this format are easier to read. This facility applies only to the tactile sense, however. The eyes can actually cover more text in less time on a broadsheet, meaning that it is visually more convenient than a tabloid. Easier to read, it bears repeating, and not to handle. If economy of time and visual effort were the reader's principal concerns, then *ABC* would be enormously inconvenient. But if it is overall handling and page-turning ease—disregarding the difficulty of finding what one wants to read in the paper—if, that is, we are talking about how well the paper fits on the breakfast table or how durable it is for commuters, then one would have to say, and I will say this without hesitation, that *ABC* is without a doubt the most convenient paper in the world.

The importance of the tactile aspect of a newspaper is further revealed when one considers a detail too often ignored by the managers and editors of newspapers: the quality of the paper used. Journalists should realize that while they are selling information, it comes wrapped in a physical package. This is not to imply that we blindly accept the maxim that the medium is the message. But we could

---

2. A Madrid daily of long standing, traditionally taking a monarchist line.—TRANS.

very well parody McLuhan by saying that the medium is also the massage insofar as senses such as touch are taken up, as indeed they should be in any discussion of a style of communication.

But let us return to the principal theme of this chapter. For a newspaper the relation between language and image generates two basic lines of exploration. One, which we might consider the more traditional line, resides in the analysis of the written word, or the text of a newspaper, to everything else: photographs, illustrations, cartoons, advertising, and headlines. These latter items are more often considered as graphic symbols than conveyors of verbal information.

The other way to look at the above-mentioned relation is to consider the newspaper itself in its whole and coherent image, as an overall symbol of the kind of messages it will send. Information professionals rarely take this perspective; its abandonment by the traditional press in our country has been particularly irritating. Here the goal of creating a newspaper as a *coherent whole* has been largely discarded for a mere juxtaposition of messages displaying no more intent or continuity than the rank enumeration of its pages.

We will attempt, albeit superficially, to address both these views, bringing into the discussion some theoretical questions and a description of the answers the Spanish press offers to them.

From Meaning to Symbol

Structural analysis allows messages to be divided into their literal and symbolic components, produced either denotatively or connotatively. Denotative meaning is simply the accepted definition of a word or image. Connotation deals with the subjective evocations of the sender and receiver of a message. This seemingly abstruse distinction is essential for newspapers to make. The same word will take on quite different meanings and suggestiveness when published by, say, *El Alcázar* or *Diario 16*.[3] A newspaper plays with the very image its readers have formed of it. Evocations also vary according to the collective emotional texture surrounding a word. "Basque," for example, is nothing more than the denomination of a specific ethnic group, but the word acquires meanings of political repression, a constitutional problem, fear, xenophobia, enemy, disorder, injustice, terrorist, revolutionary, or political prisoner according to who says it, where it is said, and who reads it.

Because of this, whether consciously or not, newspapers do strive to create their own narrative style. To be clean and concise is not enough: a style must also respond to the overall relation between a newspaper and its readers. Out of this process a recodification of language emerges, specific to each daily and the community it has targeted for itself.

For a long time, journalists—including those who work for the most sophisticated media—have cultivated these *special languages* only in their lexical dimension. In Spanish newspapers, and even in magazines, photographs generally lack a system of explicit message codification. They usually end up as mere illustrations of a story. The practice of graphic journalism is essentially nonexistent in daily

---

3. Two Madrid dailies, the former ultra-conservative and the latter liberal-left.— TRANS.

papers, perhaps because of the devastating power of television in this area. This fact is all the more illogical in Spain because the predominant print technology for newspapers here is really a graphic one—the archaic rotogravure press. It is becoming increasingly difficult to find this method used outside of our country. The invention of offset printing and improvements in typographical impressions have made this method obsolete. Today it produces papers that look more like dime store sticker books than anything else. Technology that in its day had appeared to be an almost revolutionary journalistic discovery, as a means for developing a graphic code of communication, has degenerated to this.

Rotogravure is such a restricting technology that it led some of Spain's most important dailies to institute a very curious practice: they actually do two—a first and second front page on the inside and outside faces of the first sheet.[4] The only apparent reason this practice continues is that it is great for advertising if the paper can keep up its circulation. In every other respect, aside from the quality of photographic reproduction, rotogravure is most inconvenient.

But things are not much better for newspapers that combine photographs and copy. I have said before and will repeat here that a specific style of graphic journalism has not yet been developed. Although it is difficult to decide which are the most poorly taught subjects in our schools of

---

4. The practice of two front pages, with lots of news photos and display ads, probably evolved to take full advantage of rotogravure's superior capacity to reproduce photographs, and to justify the expense of the better quality newsprint used in the production of the outside sheet of tabloids such as *ABC.*—Trans.

[14]

journalism and information science, this one certainly has to rank right up there with the worst. It has always surprised me that writing and graphics are separate areas of concentration in these schools. This tendency to make grammarians of future journalists and scene directors of press photographers is very much a product of the ridiculous pretentiousness of our journalism schools. Spanish intellectual myth making is the major danger looming over this aspect of our craft. Such academic wheel spinning ends up generating shoddy and small-minded results: the Spanish press does not manage image in any sense of that word. From photographs to layout, through the choice of a particular typeface or cartoon, there is no coherence between the intentions of the writer and the visual image of the newspaper, between content and its physical representation.

With respect to photography, our efforts at *El País* have met with almost complete failure. If in the beginning there was any real attempt to combine journalistic writing and photojournalism in the paper, our professionals' lack of training—and those most lacking wielded pens and not cameras—soon put an end to that endeavor. Journalists in Spain do not receive any visual education; there is no understanding of the power of image as an expressive tool in the reporting of news. Photographs are merely illustrations in our newspapers; they serve as accompaniments, and rarely as anything more.

Returning to our previous line of reasoning, it can be said that our paper's photographs seldom go beyond their literal meanings to tap the power of symbolic evocation. *A picture is worth a thousand words* is basically an unknown or misunderstood maxim among the majority of our journalists.

The absence of coherence between written and graphic language is, well, galling.

Cartoons and comics comprise an exception to this state of affairs. Picture stories and jokes are good examples of what the experts call multiple messages (those sent across various combinations of channels). A newspaper itself is an example of multiple messages, or at least it should be. At the very least it is one of multiple massages: where sight and touch, verbal and symbolic language, and definitions and connotations combine for the purpose of communicating to the reader. It is difficult to find a better example of the combination of text and image than that offered by cartoonists. Even when the censorship of the Franco regime was at its strictest, *Mingote* was an oasis of freedom and ingenuity in *ABC*. During the days of virtual rejection of the press by public opinion, he along with *Forges, Chummy Chúmez, Máximo, Perich, Peridis,* and many others made possible the miracle of communication. Stories and cartoons of this sort play heavily on the evocative and, therefore, on the subjectivity of their readers. In order for a reader to be able to enter the world of the newspaper cartoonist he must share important assumptions, be aware of the social climate, and in general be in tune with what is going on. Finally, these cartoonists form a coherent and compact identity with the daily in which they appear. It becomes almost impossible to think of *Forges* outside the context of *Informaciones,* or of *Mingote* anywhere but in *ABC,* or of *Peridis* not doing his cartoons for *El País.*

On the other hand, the use of illustrations is quite rare in our newspapers. They are handled as senselessly as photographs. Clearly, one of a newspaper's most difficult tasks is to make accurate graphs and adequate maps that at the same time prove understandable to most of its readers. Newspapers rarely succeed in this. A struggle is on to incorporate something from the world of illustration into a few magazines and Sunday supplements, but not much has been accomplished here, either. Perhaps some economic reasons are to blame: graphic artists find it more profitable to work in advertising. But again, one might well find the cause to be the lack of faith in image as an expressive element on the part of our journalists.

As a result of all this, the visual impact of our daily press is found almost exclusively in advertising and in headlines. Regarding the former, one has to say that considerable chaos reigns in the debate on its meaning and impact for newspapers. While ad agencies possess capable specialists, designers, and technicians—professionals, that is, who are able to build their work around a specific and concrete theme—their ads then appear in our newspapers without any input from the editorial staff. I do not know of the existence of a true commercial graphics department at any of our newspapers. These departments are common at English-language dailies, even at regional and local ones.

The mixture of news and advertising produces a veritable mosaic effect. The reader is obliged to manage his attention carefully as he wades through the paper. Press professionals are accustomed to ignoring the ads. Senior editors, when reviewing the pages of their respective papers, are rarely aware of the contents of the ads. The appeal of advertising imagery, studied in great detail to maximally attract reader attention, acts paradoxically as both a system of selection and rejection for the reader. In any case, ads are the principal occupiers of nontextual space in newspapers and magazines. In the latter they even become sources of beauty or points at which one can take restful breaks from reading. Nonetheless, seldom does a publication achieve an advertising image coherent with editorial content. Ad agencies develop massive and uniform campaigns for all the media in a somewhat mystifying manner, because it does not make sense to think—in spite of the narrow nature of the Spanish reader market—that the same person will read publications of different and opposed interests. The search for an advertising image well integrated within the editorial slant of a publication occasionally succeeds only with the so-called erotic magazines. In experiences of this kind, our newspapers are virgins.

From a merely visual point of view, advertising does tend to distort the conception of a newspaper. It is very difficult to go against the tastes and desires of an advertising client who always has preconceived notions as to how the ads should look. If on top of that, sales are doing well, it becomes virtually impossible to convince him that a change in the ads would reduce reader rejection within a particular publication, thereby increasing its overall appeal. Once again the blame for this rests more squarely on the shoulders of the newspaper professionals. They have habitually looked at advertising agents with undisguised disdain. In reality this attitude is nothing more than an unjustified, intellectually chauvinistic posture. A newspaper is the totality of its contents and not a list of newsy telegrams or a collection of essays. Advertising in newspapers is a necessity, and not just a financial one. The ever-popular saying that newspapers without ads are dreary may be somewhat vulgar, but it certainly does reflect an objective fact. McLuhan points out that ads, after all, are news too—the *good news* that papers bring to readers. Except in rare instances, readers very strongly reject newspapers without advertising, even if they do not read them or are actually bothered by their presence. All too often, editors forget that they are responsible for the entire publication—the appearance and content of the ads included—and not just the production of the editorial staff. A reader buys a finished product at the newsstand, and this product must have an appropriate advertising image.

Headlines complete the list of visual elements of a newspaper. In the best dailies, they receive very sober management. The attention of their editorial staffs is occupied with actual content and column width. Here, a specific and immediate visual impact distinct from the overall impact of the paper itself is not sought. However, things are different on the pages of the more popular dailies: headlines are visual images before they become conceptual expressions.

Newspapers have a traditional system of signaling the relative importance of news by varying the column width of the headlines. Popular newspapers, on the other hand, create their headlines for visual impact, and this effect dominates the collection of materials on the rest of the page. Punctuation, accent marks, capital and lower case letters all have their meaning in this kind of headline. It seeks to impress the reader not verbally but visually. One commonly finds this kind of headline practice in the Spanish press, as, for example, in Emilio Romero's *Pueblo*.[5] Its symbolic and

---

5. Emilio Romero is a well-known staunch conservative political columnist in Madrid, and he currently writes for *El Alcázar*. He is not exactly well loved. A promoter of limited change within Francoism before Franco's death, he became a leading

evocative power is enormous. And it is probably the only area in which our press can correlate image simply and effectively with content.

Every newspaper has a logo at the top of the front page. It ceases to be conceptualized by the reader, and serves only as a symbol or brand image. This is the only thing that explains how a name so inane as *ABC* could survive and prosper in the Spanish press. Can you imagine a newspaper coming out with the name *OPQ*, for example? Names of newspapers are not read, they are simply seen. They are differentiating insignias, factory trademarks, nothing more.

Before putting *EL PAIS* out on the street some academicians who were helping us write a small style manual insisted that we needed to put the accent mark above the *I* in *PAIS* in order to break up the diphthong. Some of the graphics people working on the logo produced a study in support of this recommendation. It showed that of the hundreds of people tested, none had written EL PAIS in capital letters or without the accent mark.[6] Reading ease also required that only the first letter in each word be cap-

advocate of a return to Francoism after the democratic transition. *El Alcázar* came out in support of the military leaders of the coup attempt of February 23, 1981 (discussed in note 3 in chap. 9), and continued its support even after King Juan Carlos came out strongly against them. Like *Pueblo* (for which Cebrián worked as a senior editor until 1968), *El Alcázar* is heavily into evocative visuals. In 1982 on my last day of a four-month stay in Madrid, I bought a copy of the paper. Its cover pages were plastered with huge photos of cracked and drying land, and for those who didn't quite get the point of the photos, the captions clearly stated that under Franco there were no droughts.—TRANS.

6. I.e., they wrote *El País*. In 1986 Mr. Cebrián informed us that the newspaper had recently appointed an ombudsman, and that its readers' first victory using that institution was to get the accent mark put back into the logo to break up the diphthong. Within a year, however, the accent mark was again removed.—TRANS.

italized. With respect to visual comfort, these observations were definitely on the mark, but they did not serve our needs for a certain visual image. We always felt that the name EL PAIS would be seen and not read: it has iconic meaning—as do the names of all newspapers—and not literal meaning. No one stops to ponder the content of a logo; everyone identifies those letters with a specific newspaper. Of the more than one hundred thousand letters I have received since the newspaper came out, only a handful have called for the accent mark in the logo.

A Coherent Whole

Text, photographs, drawings, advertisements, and headlines are the raw material with which a newspaper is made. But a newspaper is not just a mixture of this material. Rather, each element should contribute to the overall informative message the paper wants the reader to receive. The form of newspapers, the structure of their sections, the size of their photos and headlines, the color of their ink and the expressiveness of their ads all shape the first basic impressions of their readers. This happens well before the effect of their selection and treatment of the news sinks in. Page layout, which in reality is the final visualization of the product before its manufacture, is a very important step in the planning of a daily. Layout editors should be journalists also, because they need recourse to professional canons when it comes time to evaluate the informative materials they work with. They frequently try to be artists, too. In fact, there are some excellent painters among them, and they try to bring some of their creativity into the making of the paper. Nevertheless, the imaginations of these people should be kept under control. Newspapers do not have problems of creativity but of coherence. Contrary to popular belief, it is not good taste, or beauty, or visual or formal equilibrium that facilitates communication most. Rather, it is that coherence alluded to before between the emitted message, its physical layout, and the immediate evocations the image of the newspaper stimulates in the reader.

This focus on the newspaper as an integral whole, not as the sum or juxtaposition of its elements, but as the expression of a previous intent, can perhaps be better illustrated with examples from our brief experience at *El País*. As it was a new daily, we had the chance to do some experimenting without disorienting our nonexistent readership. In the three months prior to its introduction a team of almost thirty journalists worked on two fundamental tasks: to compose a first and incomplete but in any case usable *manual of style,* and to create a prototype in accordance with that journalistic style. Many of the things that came to make up the newspaper may have been erroneous, but almost nothing was the result of personal arbitrariness or chance. Some seemingly minor decisions took hours and even days to thrash out. Some examples of this were the locations of the business, labor, and international sections, the advisability of the business pages also encompassing labor news, the variable location of the opinion pieces, and the placing of the events calendar and the classified ads in the middle of the paper. With each step in this process we went further afield from the standard conceptions of Spanish dailies, and took apart principles rarely challenged, such as whether the most interesting news—in this case the national political news—should perforce run on the first pages. What guided us in this process were essentially pragmatic criteria: the reader's ability to find any section immediately, easy identification of highly specialized sections. . . . There was also a general criterion: the desire to make a newspaper that was to be read in its entirety, or at least one that could be so read.

When it came to the actual graphic design, these pragmatic principles got quite complicated. When it came out, many people said they thought it was a "pretty" newspaper. Actually, in adopting a physical format this was the least of our concerns. Our first concern was with the selection of a typeface. Its size was chosen exclusively for visual comfort, and the spacing of the text came basically from the exigencies of industrial production. On another matter, it appeared to us that the flashy layout of some other dailies was getting out of hand: what with their plethora of arrows, lead paragraphs and multitude of typefaces, their papers looked more like highways plastered with billboards and traffic signals. There had to be a simple system for identification and evaluation without provoking that kind of chaos. In addition, the demands of photocomposition would be met more easily if the whole newspaper, absolutely all of it, was composed primarily with the same kind of typeface and a standardized column width. That then allowed us to reserve a different typeface for ads, so that readers could more easily distinguish between what was and was not informative copy. The decision was similar regarding headlines. We looked for a strong clear type that would allow the eyes to scan them without having to pause long to know what they contained. We decided to use lowercase letters in the headlines because they are easier to read. We also set them flush left because we found the eye works less than for centered headlines. We also decided to write the titles of opinion pieces in cursive type and to center them so that they could be distinguished more rapidly from the news.

We drastically limited the possible size of headlines and established page designs that would facilitate quick makeup. Now at *El País* the pages are laid out before they are written, and the writers produce their copy thinking not only about what they are going to say but also how they will make it look. For the sports and culture pages we selected a separate typeface for the headlines to accentuate the different treatment these sections get. We also allowed for the possibility of wider headlines and sought a larger and more expressive photographic presence for the sports pages.

Some of these plans were put into practice and some not, but the important point from the experience is drawn not so much from the actual results as from the fact that a set of industrial and journalistic criteria guided us in the design of *El País*. We did not try to make a "pretty" paper, but one that was easy to read and to produce. And we ended up with a beautiful paper.

I have chosen to spend a long time—perhaps abusively long—on this example because I felt it was a simple and useful way to illustrate my argument for the need to establish a sound relationship between written language and the overall image of a newspaper. I believe it is one of the subjects least broached by the Spanish press.

A sterilized journalistic style that does not promote a correlation with visual images can lose a large part of its expressive capacity. At the same time, the use of a language that does not allow for the plastic possibilities of expression that a newspaper really has, or of a language that is not—or not easily—amenable to design and manufacturing requirements, would be an aberration.

The achievement of a union of language and image, and the attentive study by journalists of the graphic potential a newspaper possesses, can only redound to the benefit of everyone.

FIESTAS + MINISTROS +
PUENTES + PROFESORES +
HUELGAS + VACACIONES = √

Chapter 3

Journalism as a Profession

When at the age of fifteen I informed my father of my desire to become a journalist, he said of course, but on the condition that I also get a degree in something—else.[1] My father was also a journalist, of solid standing in the profession, but evidently he did not see his as the best of all worlds. I always hate to cite myself in anything I write, but on this occasion I believe this little anecdote is appropriate because it illustrates the low social esteem in which the humane and intellectual functions of journalists are held. Even now one hears prestigious colleagues say without batting an eyelash that "this is a profession one should abandon as soon as possible." The world of letters for the creative, and of politics for the active—these are not infrequently the real horizons in the subconscious minds of young journalists as they start out.

---

1. Cebrián entered the university at age fifteen and took a degree in philosophy.— TRANS.

And many of those who have no other aspirations than to die between the press plates or serenaded by the sounds of teletype plainly confess that journalism, though they like it, is not really a profession but a trade.

Distinguishing which intrinsic and social characteristics an activity has to possess in order to be considered a profession, or knowing how to draw the line between the craftsmen of the past and the colleagues of today, is at times a rather tricky endeavor. But to my way of thinking, two conditions are necessary for one to be able to talk of the existence of a profession: the recognition by its practitioners of a set of common interests, and the development of a specific educational and internship program for future practitioners. Both conditions are unequivocally met in the industrially developed states, including—and this is our case—those states in which the importance of public opinion as a pillar of the social edifice is not recognized. But journalism as a profession is actually a recent phenomenon. It began in the United States around 1920 and in Europe after World War II.[2] Thus one frequently finds, even on the staffs of the most modern and evolved newspapers, journalists from schools of journalism in constant conflict with "self-made men," resulting in the perpetuation of arguments over whether journalists are born or made.

I believe it was Camilo José Cela[3] whom I heard on some

---

2. John Hohenberg, *El periodista profesional* (México: Editorial Letras, n.d.), 17ff. (Published in the United States as *The Professional Journalist* [New York: Holt, Rinehart and Winston, 1961].)

3. Camilo José Cela (1916–) has been a famous figure in the world of Spanish letters since the publication in 1942 of his novel *The Family of Pascual Duarte, La Familia de Pascual Duarte* (Madrid: Editorial Aldecoa, 1942), a work that was

occasion say that no one is simply born these days, but rather made in the course of time and through years of education. This is not to deny that there exist in people certain inherent or genetic traits that make them in each case more capable or comfortable in certain activities. Vocation, whether a gift from heaven or from the state of consciousness, continues to hold conceptual weight among us. But I do not know why those who have creative professions insist upon denying the necessity of a serious and structured education. The journalist, like the medical doctor, the architect, the painter, plumber, or professional speculator, is someone who is obviously made. The spark of genius needs to be fanned with education if we wish it to catch fire.

The old reporters, those who began as "gofers" bringing coffee to the staff or who just hung around looking for a little money to live on while they continued to write their poetry, feel a logical rejection of anything which is not autodidactic. "Everyone from those schools of journalism wants to start out as a foreign correspondent or an editorial writer. No one wants the police beat," they usually say. And they insist that there is no better teacher than life itself, that is,

---

originally banned by the Franco regime but which received such acclaim and such diffusion in Spain through pirated editions that the regime finally backed down and allowed its publication in Spain. The novel marks for many the renewal of serious literary production in Spain after the devastation of the Spanish Civil War (1936–39). Cela worked for a time as a censor for the regime and in the 1980s came under some fire for his Francoist past. In a beautiful essay in his book *Crónicas de mi país* (Madrid: PRISA, 1985), Cebrián defends Cela by saying that there is a consistency and unique insight in his attitude toward political life, that this perspective is part and parcel of his brilliant literary work, and that the criticisms against his Francoist past were petty at best. During the 1980s Cela has been a member of parliament (appointed by Juan Carlos) and his columns have appeared regularly in *El País*.—TRANS.

than actually working for a newspaper. But the truth is that when new graduates come out with their hot degrees ready to change the whole world, they rarely find jobs. Wherever they go they find out right away that they need previous work experience, because editors usually lack confidence in the education they receive at journalism schools or at the university. "How am I going to get the experience if no one hires me?" the young usually argue. "And why did I waste four or five years studying if this isn't enough to get me a job?" add the ones most fiercely jealous of their academic efforts.

In reality there is a worldwide battle between the academic journalists—to give them a name—and the self-taught. Nevertheless, no one will deny that to do well today, a journalist needs a high level of intellectual preparation. However, this fact alone does not tell us whether there exists a specific program of studies that, once completed, will allow one to call oneself a journalist in the same way one calls oneself a doctor or an engineer. The greater problem is that almost none of the good journalists have gone on to teach their profession. Unlike what occurs for other professions, training in the classroom instead of the newsroom teaches journalists very little of what they need to know. And with rare exceptions, research—which is the primary reason for the existence of universities—is not much done by journalists. They instead prefer to study concrete problems useful to the profession, but which do not rigorously investigate the institution itself. One may find great columnists, for example, who are experts in law, politics, science, or history, but they almost never deal with specifically journalistic issues. All too frequently it is the worst of the professionals who find refuge for their unproductiveness and inefficiency in a school of journalism. There are innumerable examples of this all over the world.

Despite all that, one can now say quite confidently that there does exist a specific body of knowledge on journalism that would allow it to be considered a profession. By this I mean that the profession has a concrete and specific technique, which has nothing to do on the one hand with literary virtuosity, or on the other with that necessary cultural preparation all journalists should have. The problem is to figure out a plan of studies to cover these techniques. Here the bibliography is large, but this is probably not the proper place to sort through that maze of erudition. Perhaps, however, it is an appropriate time to point out the absurd focus we in this country have on the matter, a focus that has produced one of the most strikingly ridiculous of all the incredible results to come out of our mismanaged university system. I am referring to the case of the so-called School of Information Sciences established at the Universidad Complutense de Madrid in 1966, out of which came our first university graduates in journalism. This school is one of the best—meaning worst—examples of how not to approach the study of journalism. What perhaps occurred here was a confluence of two separate problems, both having their origins in our archaic and obsolete social structures. The first is the anachronistic and limited concept of what the university is to us, where the goal is not research and education but a pure formalism in the granting of degrees. The other is the excess of bureaucratic controls over a profession whose essence is the freedom to inform and be critical. Therefore, under the guise of an obvious need to produce journalists, an entelechy of a school program was constructed in which the purpose was to emulate the humanities as much as possible, but not to recover the lost metaphysics of the Linotype and the Polaroid. Pressured by the painful reality of an often poorly educated and informed professional class, the schools of journalism and of information science have been gradually turned into places that attempt to give students a broad cultural base—which the journalist by then should have acquired in high school or in another academic program—while simultaneously making mythology out of the knowledge of simple reporting techniques. These techniques could be taught to even the slowest of those who aspire to the profession in about three months.

The picture is not totally bleak, however. The existence of public entities that are, at least in theory, dedicated to the teaching of a profession has encouraged a generation of students with a vocational attraction to journalism, in contrast to those for which it has been a secondary interest, or to others having easy connections but little interest or ability. These same youngsters, on whose shoulders is beginning to rest the bulk of the responsibility for the Spanish press and public opinion, are the ones who get frustrated by incredible spectacles such as the School of Information offering Ph.D.s to people who want nothing more—and nothing less—than to become good journalists, reporting with veracity and precision.

I cannot resist the temptation, probably obscene, of reproducing as an example of this problem a paragraph from a weighty tome entitled *The Information Industry,* from which my unfortunate colleagues are condemned to learn.[4] On page 94 it reads:

---

4. Pedro J. Pinillos, *La empresa informativa: Prensa, radio, cine y televisión* (Madrid: Ediciones del Castillo, 1975).

The correlation, that is to say, the degree of mutual relation existing between various phenomena, shows us that if we call [Y] newspaper circulation, X_1 the cultural index, X_2 purchasing power, and X_3 provincial income, and we carry out a series of operations, they will yield us a coefficient very close to unity, which indicates the existence of a strong relation between newspaper circulation and the above-mentioned indicators.

The coefficients obtained are:

$$R_{01} = \frac{48\Sigma yx_1 - (\Sigma y)(\Sigma x_1)}{\sqrt{48\Sigma y^2 - (\Sigma y)^2}\sqrt{48\Sigma x_1^2 - (\Sigma x_1)^2}} = 0.9767683$$

which is the correlation coefficient existing between newspaper circulation and the cultural index,

$$R_{02} = \frac{48\Sigma yx_2 - (\Sigma y)(\Sigma x_2)}{\sqrt{48\Sigma y^2 - (\Sigma y)^2}\sqrt{48\Sigma x_2^2 - (\Sigma x_2)^2}} = 0.9504391$$

which gives us the coefficient between circulation and purchasing power [, and]

$$R_{03} = \frac{48\Sigma yx_3 - (\Sigma y)(\Sigma x_3)}{\sqrt{48\Sigma y^2 - (\Sigma y)^2}\sqrt{48\Sigma x_3^2 - (\Sigma x_3)^2}} = 0.9504391$$

Furthermore, I must point out that this paragraph is by no means unique. The book is plagued with similar examples. Neither are we dealing with a case of a single professor or a specific course. With very honorable exceptions in some specific instances, from top to bottom and beginning to end the journalistic career—which I can't help but love, as it is my own—has in our country become a succession of academic and administrative disasters.

Perhaps a major share of the blame belongs to the professional journalists themselves. We did not attempt or even know how to have our say in course development or in the analysis of just what kind of thing a university-level school of journalism should be. But be that as it may, the intolerable fiction that the Spanish university system of today trains journalists is one that should be laid to rest once and for all.

Paradoxically, the study of journalism is quite well structured and developed in many countries. Hundreds of specialized schools and institutes distributed among universities all over the world demonstrate just how specialized one can get in the training of a journalist for his work. The first school of this genre at the university level was established in the United States—in Missouri—in 1908, although by then other U.S. schools had similar departments on an experimental basis. Forty years later, the number had grown to over seventy in that country. It was no coincidence in 1912 that a journalist, Joseph Pulitzer, and not a professor, was the founder of the most famous and important school of journalism in the world at Columbia University, a school that operates strictly at the graduate level. What would the creator of those famous prizes for literature and journalism say today if he found someone trying to take his (Graduate) School of Journalism and rename it the School of Information Science? Someone put it well when they said that the sublime, when it really isn't, turns out to be histrionic.

But apart from these questions, structured education does, as I said, facilitate the selection of vocationally authentic journalists, ready to consider themselves practitioners of a profession. In most countries, the existence of schools of journalism precedes chronologically that of journalistic unions and associations. A few years after the schools of journalism are started, the latter begin to organize to defend the professional interests of journalists against editors and newspaper owners. One can say that it has been only since World War II that editorial staff unions have been capable of claiming and defending their rights, even when those claimed were not economic or salary-related.

The mark of the trade for journalists is that although they feel they are a salaried class—with all the "proletarian" baggage that goes with that term—they consider themselves a specific kind of intellectual. Because newspaper companies are idea enterprises, the professional interests of the editorial staff often revolve around issues on a moral plane rather than about the workplace or labor conditions. In the English-speaking countries where freedom of expression is acknowledged as a deeply rooted social principle, organized pressure to maintain information independence has been, perhaps because it was not so necessary, less strong as a rule than in other European nations. Things that a French or an Italian journalist—not to mention a Spanish journalist—have been spending years trying to achieve on ethical issues surrounding the control of the press are guaranteed at the outset to all professional journalists in England and the United States. This is not to say that the latter have solved all their problems, but that they are rather faced with a quite different set of circumstances. In America, for example, there exists a traditional separation between opinion pages and those dedicated to the news. While in the latter pages the independence of journalists is almost complete, the companies and their editorial management reserve the right to set the lines of the former. Organized protest over moral issues by journalists probably started in France. But what the French began to struggle for almost twenty-five years ago—recognition of the responsibility and power of newsmen with respect to the content of newspapers—was something that if not completely achieved, was then in an advanced stage toward achievement in the United States and in the United Kingdom. The French movement crystalized into famous "journalist associations," the first of which being that of *Le Monde*. Their founding charter states that their objective is to guarantee that journalists themselves "assume the intellectual and moral responsibilities of informing." For their own part, American and English journalists have spent most of their time trying to get salary increases and more job security than in the fight for a freedom of the press, which they believe to be already won and respected. Only in the sixties did they begin to look at the particular features of their problem when they realized that there was in fact a class of journalists—the influential members of the editorial staff—who in effect were assuming the responsibility of making editorial policy. Rarely did the foot soldiers of the profession have access to these kinds of decisions. In any case, the creation of a professional conscience that makes journalists as a group feel responsible, before society, for the freedom of the press is a relatively recent achievement around the world. It is not off the mark to think that new battles will take place on this terrain, particularly in Spain. The establishment of "editorial statutes," like political pacts between companies and their editorial staffs, could well be the appropriate answer to this kind of problem.

Our country's situation is even more complex. Freedom

of the press was not objectively recognized by the Spanish political structure during the Franco regime, and Spanish journalists therefore became belligerents in the struggle for its conquest. The activities of journalists inevitably became politicized against a political system that was repressive and did not respect a basic right of the profession: the freedom to practice it. At the same time, as a result of the civil war and of the subsequent years of censorship and direct state control of the sector, "amateurism" continues to plague Spanish journalism. For this reason, the older generations look distrustfully at the younger journalists. In spite of this, a feeling of unity among Spanish journalists in the quest for a guaranteed freedom of the press for professionals grows day by day. The staffs of all the great Spanish dailies are full of young journalists with stupendous preparation and enthusiasm for their work, and who through the Press Associations and Unions of Journalists are working for recognition of professional dignity and against impediments to reporting. To a large degree, the best Spanish dailies are made by these young journalists. This is not to say that journalism is a religion to them—they pay little attention to religions of any kind. They hold it simply as a bona fide profession. The conditions of high juridical uncertainty they have to face daily take their toll. At the risk of sounding clannish, I must acknowledge the high price Spanish journalists have to and do pay in defense of an ideal of independence, and of a vision of the role of information in a free society.

Freedom of the press is not an isolated concept, rather it is an expression, effect and cause simultaneously, of a larger and more defined group of freedoms that pertain to those societies called democratic. The greatness and pettiness of the journalistic profession resides precisely in this: in being—without any mythification or falsehood—a real servant of the interests of a people, which in the case of a newspaper are its readers. So although a lot of the invective thrown at journalists may be justified, the important role played by the press in the democratization of the country should nonetheless be recognized.

A well-defined education and a set of corporate interests are thus the essential characteristics of any profession. They are also a set of problems attracting the attention of journalists throughout the world.

Finally, we must admit that journalism is a difficult profession, and one not entirely free of sins. It is full of insane and illustrious people, of people who want to be saints and generals, politicians and artists. Some of these are desirous of knowing everything down to the last detail, of seducing women, of mingling indiscriminately with gamblers and ministers, trying to play the powerful, the spy, the writer. . . . There are among us adventurers, bureaucrats, pencil pushers, clowns, consummate pontificators, deadbeats, and the occasional blasphemer. "In sum," says Jean-Louis Servan-Schreiber,

> even if their talent is not much above average, even if they are sportswriters, every journalist considers himself to be a bit like the intellectual. Worker without tools, his professional capital is completely under his hat. Although his boss may fire him, he cannot take away his instruments of production. Of all the salaried professions it is the one which offers more intellectual, creative, and independent initiative.[5]

---

5. Jean-Louis Servan-Schreiber, *El poder de informar* (Barcelona: Dopesa, 1973). (Published in English as *The Power to Inform* [New York: McGraw-Hill, 1974].)

Perhaps these characteristics are what so often cause con-fusion amongst journalists themselves about the true nature of the work they do. Perhaps from them come the concurrent attraction and rejection of the press by society. For this reason more will have to be written someday about the problems and frustrations the people of the press in our country encounter daily in carrying out, if only for their own sense of dignity, the function for which they feel called. But for those who know, as I do, the misery and joy the news-room elicits, and who have spent over half their lives in the midst of this crazy and captivating profession, journalism will continue to be a passionate profession, impossible to leave, a profession in which one will have to die with his boots on.

EL PAIS

EL MIRROR

EL MONDE

EL BILD

EL CORRIERE

EL TIMES

LA PRAVDA

EL POST

El País

Chapter 4

Letters to the Editor

For a number of years now I have spent a few hours each day reading material often much more instructive and passionate than any book or magazine—the letters to the editor that I receive each morning in my office at *El País*.

In times past, reading the letters section of our newspapers was for me a painful and disconcerting matter. They really did not exist, because hardly anyone felt like writing a letter to the editor. I used to turn green with envy when I looked through the pages of the British press, where the letters sections are the most regal, and where in my earliest days I got used to seeing the signature of a Bertrand Russell or a Churchill mixed in with that of a fruit seller in Covent Garden or a lady from Manchester. I supposed back then that this was the result of an evolved British society, something we could not even dream of in a country like ours. I believe that all Spanish journalists will have to confess to writing fictitious letters to the editor on more than one occasion because, as I said, there were times when real letters were very rare beasts.

Rarer still were letters that merited publishing. To some this was a clear indication of the disregard in which the Spanish press was held during the Franco dictatorship. The lack of communication between readers and their newspapers was part and parcel of the internal isolation of Spanish society itself. We suffered religious, political, social, and moral persecution, and our behavior degenerated into a set of formalized rituals that could maintain indefinitely the absurd situation in which everyone talked about everything without actually saying anything to each other. The fear of expressing oneself, out of a fear of ridicule or of the police, reached proverbial status among us. Even today the absence of sincerity in our conversations is often irritating. And we have come to substitute for interesting content a certain stupid audacity of form. The Spaniard is probably the most expressive and emotional expounder of ephemeral themes. With wind and fanfare he hopes, vainly, to cover up for the lack of any honest, consistent expression of his own ideas in his speech. Of all the liberties repressed by the Franco regime, the freedom of expression was the one most completely quashed. We could entertain the notion that the censorship and direct state control only affected the press and public expression, but the final casualties turned out to be the intimate consciousness and will of the Spanish people. The indoctrinated citizen whose reading, information, and films were strictly controlled, began to behave rather neurotically—with the scientists' pardon—with respect to anything having to do with dialogue and communication. In Madrid and Barcelona, and even in Huelva, many laughed at the sight of fleets of chartered buses and planes organized to take people to Perpignan to see *Last Tango in Paris.*

Almost no one had the fortitude to say that there was nothing funny or inane about the situation and that, above and beyond any other interpretation, a regime that forced its citizenry who were desirous of more culture than was permitted to make such long pilgrimages was, simply, a condemnable regime. For years and years we Spanish had to bring everything from *Playboy* to Marx's *Capital* across the borders clandestinely; we almost trembled at the accusing eyes of the customs officials who grabbed our copies of Lukács or Garaudy, or even of Salvador de Madariaga,[1] and fingered through them with their knowing airs. We witnessed the awful spectacle of the system's bureaucrats buying volumes in Biarritz the reading of which they themselves prohibited of Spanish citizens. We suffered the shame of seeing those who dared to think or to speak against the reigning powers jailed, persecuted, or exiled. We had to take advantage of business trips to see films; we filled the striptease joints of Pigalle and the nudist theaters of London. We were, in a word, beggars—of a little freedom to see and to hear, of some freedom to read, of the liberty that was denied us within our borders and that from beyond manip-

---

1. Salvador de Madariaga was a famous Spanish essayist who, along with many intellectuals, went into exile after the Spanish Civil War. Georg Lukács and Roger Garaudy share the distinction of having been active members of the communist parties of their respective countries of Hungary and France, prolific writers, and intellectuals whose reworkings of aspects of Marxist theory brought them great trouble from defenders of the orthodox line laid down by Moscow. They are major figures in the western European attempt to work out a more fluid, less authoritarian line of Marxist thought than that which emanated from the Soviet Union from the time of Stalin to the recent past. During the 1970s and early 1980s this independent line of thought was often called "Eurocommunism," and one of the people most closely associated with the term is Santiago Carrillo, head of the Spanish Communist Party.—TRANS.

ulated us. And at times in our imaginations and innocence we would fuse things so respectable yet so different as bare arses and democracy.

In such a state of affairs how could anyone write anything about anything? How could one ask a citizen to express himself clearly and simply if not even the journalists dared to do so? How would we demand sincerity, insight, ingenuity, and generosity from others when we journalists were ourselves lacking in these qualities? For years the only mail to the editor worth reading was written anonymously and was therefore unpublishable. There was either a letter from some Warrior of Christ the King[2] or from some Hitlerian commandos saying they were going to tear somebody to pieces, or accusations, usually unverifiable, of the corruption of some high public official. For a journalist convinced that information, and indeed the newspapers themselves, were the property of their readers, the situation was one of despair. There certainly were buyers and clients of dailies, but it appeared as if no one actually read them, as if nobody were paying attention to the messages being sent out. There was in effect a lack of communication between the newspaper and those who received it. The technocrats of Opus Dei had created a new version of the concept of *enlightened despotism*: everything for the people but without the people.[3] Everything for the people? The passage of time has

2. A militant ultraright youth organization. The religious warrior theme was also used by Franco: he called the insurgency that he helped begin in 1936 a "crusade."—TRANS.

3. Opus Dei seems to be modeled in part on a Spanish Catholic image of secretive European Masonic organizations. It was founded in 1929 by a Father José María Escrivá and was recognized by the Vatican as a secular institute in 1947. It has

given us a picture of just how feebly enlightened those developers of despotism really were. They tried unsuccessfully to bury our most cherished liberal traditions forever. But Spaniards knew how to think and read, even to read between the lines when it was necessary to do so.

Among the freedoms which we could classify as minor ones, and which we hope will never again disappear, should be included that of writing letters, judging by the large numbers now received daily at my newspaper. I have always maintained that the success of *El País,* which I should with due humility be permitted to recognize, is attributable in large part to the fact that the people in the streets have identified the fate of the newspaper with the political changes occurring in Spain. I have to add that I have derived a lot of satisfaction from my experience as its editor, but nothing has been so pleasing as opening the mail every morning.

"Writing letters means to denude oneself before the ghosts, something for which they greedily wait," said Kafka in his amorous epistles to his beloved Milena Jesenska.[4] In my opinion, there is one other kind of letter that surpasses love letters in passion and exacerbation: the political kind. It is not surprising that literature abounds with examples

---

attempted to penetrate and take over secular government and business institutions, and once controlled, to rationalize their operations. Strangely enough, this secretive organization seems to be doing battle with what some religious groups in the United States call "secular humanist" social forces, while doing its best to import U.S. business and marketing practices. If one wishes to learn the business trade in Spain today, one need look no further than the Opus-controlled schools and publishing houses. Note here the term "technocrat" used in the same breath with Opus. Opus technocrats were very influential in Spanish economic and political life from the 1960s on through to the early 1980s.—TRANS.

4. Franz Kafka, *Letter to Milena* (New York: Schocken, 1953).

of this epistolary genre. From Cicero (*To Atticus, Quintus, and Brutus*) to Montesquieu (*Persian Letters*); from Seneca (*To Lucilius*) to Quevedo (*Of the Knights of the Tenaza*); from Feijóo (*The Erudite*) to Cadalso (*Moroccan Letters*); from Larra to Valera, letters have been a pretext and vehicle for literary, political and social criticism. Even today there is a great journalist among us, Augusto Assía,[5] who uses the epistolary genre in high-circulation newspapers. One thing is certain: the directness in approach to any subject that one can take with letters have made them a valuable method, if not an easy one, for writing articles. I think that the reading of a selection of letters of a few of the authors I have cited would do wonders for more than a few of our contemporary government officials and leaders. Not because of the old saw that history is—if it ever really was—the teacher of life, but because it is frightening to contemplate how many of their criticisms for those times are relevant today, and how surely many of those writers would have been classified as subversives under Franco, and even under the new democracy. Those texts are true monuments to our shame. Among the things they show us is how little we have progressed in the development of freedom and models of coexistence.

The letters to the editor section, I believe I am not mistaken in saying, is today one of the most widely read and discussed sections of *El País*. The missives now number more than one hundred thousand since the paper's birth, which gives an idea of the dialogue that has been estab-

---

5. Cebrián refers to the famous Italian journalist.—TRANS.

lished. A strong focus on the reader is the mark of classic journalistic principles, and the competent professional's golden rule: *keep the reader in mind.* As I have already asserted, the readers are the real owners of information. We journalists are actually the administrators of someone else's property. Freedom of information is after all not the exclusive right of professional journalists, but of all citizens and the whole society. There can be no democratic state without free-flowing information, because democracy is based on universal suffrage and public opinion. But neither can newspapers be the dictators of that public opinion. It would surprise those who only follow the adventures of the press *from the outside* just how far a publication escapes the hands of its editors and staff and acquires a life of its own under the pressure of its readers' opinions. Many of the former assure us that they follow the laws of the market, by trying to say what the majority want them to say in order to sell more copies. But that's not the way it really is. Those of us who believe in the social role of our profession, and in the newspaper as a public forum, know that listening to the advice and opinions of those who read us is the only way to learn to serve them. All those absurd hours under countless crises—which make up the work of journalism—receive their greatest and final reward in the knowledge that every morning three or four hundred thousand people are going to pick up your paper and read and judge you. To not listen to what they say, or to not acknowledge their existence is not only sheer intellectual stupidity, but also the quickest way to sink a publication.

A reader of a newspaper who takes the trouble to write a letter—to protest, applaud, or suggest whatever thing, put it in an envelope, place a stamp on it and drop it in the mail, is a reader who undoubtedly feels that for better or worse the paper he's reading is his. The explicit capacity demonstrated by the Spanish who read the press to identify with or reject a paper is to me a symptom of their readiness for participation and dialogue in all its forms. Our people were neither illiterate nor poorly prepared for democracy. The Spanish, it certainly appears, are a people quite ready and willing to dialogue. They can, when appropriate, display a harsh critical sense or express themselves with tact. They are entirely able to expound their ideas with absolute normality and civility.

One writes to a newspaper for the most diverse reasons. I keep letters from political exiles, émigrés, prostitutes, terrorists, prisoners, beggars, ministers, from intellectuals, laborers, students, bullfighters, bankers, artists, priests, children, military personnel, judges, ambassadors, and gypsies. Letters that insult, eulogize, criticize, tear apart, exalt, inspire, which in every case quicken the emotions because they contain the heart, the ideas, and the feelings of someone who wants to speak and express himself. How can you calm the angry government official or the indignant politician incapable of eating his morning crow who accuses you of being tendentious, a fabricator, or a liar? What can you say to the housewife who asks for money because her husband has been laid off or fired? What can you say to the prisoner who confesses that for him your newspaper is his only source of life and hope? And how do you pacify the intellectual who is always upset because he is paid so little and is published even less? How far do you follow up on some accusation of corruption or dishonesty? And what attention do you pay to threats or to the unreasonable, to all the expressions of jubilation and pain that flood your mail every day? A newspaper is certainly not a hot line of hope, but why shouldn't it be? Here in Spain especially at this moment a newspaper has absolutely no justification for its existence if it does not place its pages at the service of the great national debates of the day. Either the press is a place to meet and discuss, a forum for liberty, or it is really nothing.

In the opinion pages of *El País,* readers have engaged in polemics on such diverse subjects as nationalities, Catalonian autonomy, the state of the economy, striptease, television, women's liberation, the Popular Alliance, abortion, divorce, and the legacy of Franco. "Why don't you people publish the economic tracts of Opus Dei?" suggests one reader. "Those of Felipe González[6] seem illiterate to me, which is not surprising since he's from Seville. If you want a socialist leader he should at least be from Madrid. Leaders should come from civilized areas."

Another reader from Barcelona proceeds to honor Franco's memory: "If Franco had been exiled after the war, how brilliantly his life and work would shine today!" A syllogism so strange it defies understanding: it's obvious that if Franco had gone into exile, it would have been because he had lost the war, in which case nothing of either his life or work would remain.

Some readers also wax poetic:

---

6. González, from Andalucia, headed the socialist party PSOE, which at the time was the principal party of opposition to the centrist coalitional government.—TRANS.

In the center of Castille,
As a grandiose symbol of the work of the Caudillo,[7]
Stands the Cross of the Fallen,
Towering over mountain,
Like the parabola of the Archangel
Where neither rain nor storm
Can bring it down.

Or they suffer from old neuroses: "Now the blood will again be spilled as terribly as before or even worse. And now the communists, the atheists, the Masons, liberals and democrats return to settle accounts with the Nation."

Spanish National Television is one of the preferred subjects. "TVE should have to be declared top secret material in view of the fact that it perfectly exemplifies what is covered under official secrets on torture and mistreatment. It is crystal clear that TVE tortures and mistreats us daily." The letter later says:

Now I don't mean to attack the Monarchy here. That's a completely different subject. I am simply denouncing the over-

---

7. *Caudillo* refers literally to Franco. The term stems from the theory of *caudillaje*, which was constructed to relate how the unity of a nation comes to be embodied in one great person. In other words, it was a theory cut by Franco's own intellectual tailors to explain Franco himself. The explanation does not go much beyond the naming stage, but at least the name itself stuck. The Cross of the Fallen is Franco's place of burial, a gigantic white cross in the mountains north of Madrid, which must be seen to be believed. Indeed, this writer seems to be groping for words to capture its tremendous visual presence. I was tempted to help him or her along by putting more of the old postal service refrain into the penultimate line . . . perhaps readers may wish to do this for themselves to capture some of the aesthetic impact of the original work.—TRANS.

whelming sadism of broadcasting and rebroadcasting footage of the Royal Family's trips over and over again. It's gotten so that now an announcement of an upcoming sojourn is enough to make one quake with fear, because it means yet another week of televisual abuse.

And the genteel correspondent ends by offering what he feels is the one solution to the problems of our idiot box: "I'm just asking that TVE have a little mercy on the Spanish people."

Then there are those who show their teeth. Regarding a joke on Girón[8] someone writes:

> As a son of a Glorious Fallen Soldier of God and Spain, Captain of the National Army, I most energetically protest the use of

---

8. Both this writer and another to come in the text refer to José Antonio Girón de Velasco (1911–), a very important minister under Franco. He was an early leader of the Spanish Falange (a Spanish fascist group discussed in the next chapter in a footnote on José Antonio Primo de Rivera). Following the Falange's paternalistic philosophy toward labor, Girón helped shape many of the Franco regime's labor and social welfare institutions. In the early 1970s he began to express his vision of life after Franco: a kind of pluralism within Francoism where one would find left-, center-, and right-Francoist tendencies engaging in "democratic" dialogue, all within the mystical safety net of something like "caudillaje." Subsequent actions by emerging political actors—including many from the regime itself—seemed to Girón to show that people were paying more attention to the notion of a democratic opening than they were to the idea of the mystical unity of Spain under a great leader. He thus turned very sharply to the right, and on April 28, 1974, published what Raymond Carr describes as an "apocalyptic manifesto" denouncing liberalism and freedom of the press. The essay came to be called a *gironazo,* and the term has generalized to describe the kind of turnabout often seen in Spanish politics in the 1970s, where one begins with an idealistic vision of what democracy might be and then becomes strongly reactionary once some of its practical consequences emerge. Gironazos usually come liberally garnished with invective. See Raymond Carr and Juan Pablo Fusi, *Spain: Dictatorship to Democracy* (London: Allen and Unwin, 1979), and Manual Vázquez Montalbán, *Diccionario del franquismo* (Barcelona: Dopesa, 1977).—TRANS.

said honorable name in such below-the-belt politicized drivel, and I suggest that from now on the author use his own dead relatives for these little jokes, or else use yours.

Some readers also get apocalyptic:

> I do not know if you are Catholic or not, or if so whether you are a traditional or modernistic one. But if you are really Catholic then forgive me for what I am about to say, because you sir do not know what the Bible and the Holy Mother Church and all its great Doctors have to say about the penalty of death. They tell us that it is not only legal, but it is prescribed by God himself. How then do you dare to infringe on the authority of God by saying that we should get rid of the death penalty?

And this writer, a parish priest in Carrilobo, Córdoba, Argentina, ends his letter by saying: "If the Spanish-speaking nations left the Catholic faith, the Catholic world would be reduced to tumbleweed."

Religion is one of the most oft-discussed themes. Concerning a news item announcing the saying of an Our Father by a cardinal at the close of the day's telecast, it occurred to one unbelieving reader to compute some figures. "I suppose," he says,

> that it would take about thirty seconds to say that prayer. Calculating that ten million of Spain's twenty-five million sets are on at that time, it would add up to three hundred million seconds a day, that is, to over eighty-three thousand hours. At 3.50 pesetas per kilowatt/hour, that would be 290,000 pesetas a day, or a total of something over a hundred million pesetas a year. Doesn't that Our Father seem a bit expensive to you?

But this communicator immediately provides his own answer, as if repentant: "Of course, the per-television tab comes to only 10.65 pesetas for each Our Father. A very modest sum."

Other writers impress by their tone as well as their message:

> According to yesterday's article on the conference given by Mr. Girón, it was reported that there took place such name-calling as traitors, midgets, etc. . . . Well, that is just the end of my patience, because using the word *midget* as an insult shows that these people do not know that interrupted growth is just the consequence of a glandular defect; its causes are only physical.

The letter ends passionately:

> There are close to a million and a half handicapped people in Spain, but our case is special. We don't ask for anything from anyone. We only wish not to end up selling matches in bars or as clowns in a circus.

Feminists also write frequently:

> In the encyclopedia of eroticism, in reference to the word *abortion,* Cela[9] reports a colloquial Castilian meaning of "ugly or unkempt woman." He is obviously unfamiliar with another Castilian colloquialism. We women use that term, at least we have since the 1960s, to describe "a poorly dressed or poorly shaped man."

---

9. Camilo José Cela.—TRANS.

She winds up her defense of the rights of women with this: "I would rather be a construction laborer or a miner than a service woman or a houseworker, as *Telva*[10] would have it."

Related to that issue is the equally popular topic of sex and eroticism. "A sane and practical sexuality is a cornerstone of the cultural and sanitary policies of a country," a writer from Santander asserts, adding:

> Is everything only politics? Aren't men and women sexual? Is it or is it not all right to masturbate? Who controls prostitution in Spain? Who controls marriage? Birth control, polygamy, feminine frigidity, the pleasure principle, incestuous relations, neuroses—are these subjects open to public opinion or are they monopolized by the Catholic Church and its bishops?

Not infrequently one gets a letter from someone wanting to discuss a problem of theirs, but who can find no better way than by writing a letter to the editor. For its dramatic and human qualities I have chosen the following from among many as an example.

> Allow me to answer a letter that appeared in this newspaper, signed by Mr. Marcelino Pulla of Cuenca, dated the 21st of November, with a title concerning homosexuality.
>
> Without wishing to sound polemical I would like to state the following very clearly: I am nineteen and homosexual. It does not give me pride to say this, as the writer believes it does, but neither does it embarrass me to say it. What you have said in

---

10. A women's magazine.—TRANS.

your letter, Mr. Pulla, has hurt me considerably, and not only me, I believe ... you consider us some kind of monster from which all should keep their distance and who should hide themselves, or at least shut up and go on as if who knows how. I do not believe that many are proud to be homosexual, but I also don't believe we should shut ourselves away. I, and many more like myself, had a very difficult time until I met other people who were like me. I felt alone; I thought I was the only one who felt this way, because when we realize what we are as we develop our sense of reason, we lose our sense of closeness with our parents and family. We don't wish to hurt them, but we know that if we tell them anything they will suffer because they cannot understand what makes us feel sadness, and if we try to share our joys it too would only cause them pain. This is why we remain alone, and why when I met others like myself I felt the world open its doors to me. There are not just two or three of us, but many thousands, and if you don't believe me just take a walk through our cafes and bars, ... although I believe you won't take the time to do it, because we frighten you, embarrass you, or something. It appears to worry you that your children could be our friends. But I will tell you I have many friends of the kind you would call normal, just like your children. They understand us and we go out together as would any other friends. I go out with them and their girlfriends and they consider me a normal human being, although with a different inclination, which itself is not about to cause them to leave their girlfriends to go to bed with me. I work as an administrative aide and my male and female colleagues know what I am because I told them, not because they noticed anything. Not one of them has ever avoided me or not helped me. ... Finally I will say that I belong to no association of homosexuals nor will I. I don't believe in that.

An editorial on autonomy and nationalities spawned a furious debate. On that occasion—and for the same reasons—I had to put up with accusations of being a red and a fascist, depending who was proffering the label. It must be admitted that passions were really unleashed by the piece. A resident of Soria went off on his own particular tangent in the dialogue:

> We are fed up with our province being used as a museum and summer playground, of our workers being paid less than their cohorts in Barcelona, of our natural wealth being polluted by a nuclear power plant, of our savings being invested in other regions like Catalonia and the Basque Country.

But criticism is not enough; solutions must be put forth:

> Therefore we have founded a party or movement or whatever they call them now: the Party for Sorian Autonomy (PAS), which is in favor of an Autonomous Soria within a free and autonomous Castille.

As one can see, the average Spaniard's capacity for ingenuity and playfulness is tremendous. It is sometimes a good idea to doubt the innocence or bad intentions in these letters. Where we believe we see irony the writer may have been serious, and vice versa.

I have offered these examples to show how entertaining my work can sometimes get. I do, of course, get some more serious and more dramatic letters. And also more important ones—which is not to say that any of these formerly unpublished ones are not also important.

Not a few writers complain that they have written two, three, or four letters to the editor without ever seeing one published. "It sure would make me happy to see myself in *El País*," one of them implores for the fifth time, while another bitterly complains: "Now I can't even trust *El País*. You people only publish what you want." An English publisher has come out with the best letters to the *Times* from 1900 to 1980.[11] Among them one can find the signatures of Arthur Conan Doyle, Neville Chamberlain, Bernard Berenson, Winston Churchill, H. G. Wells, T. S. Eliot, George Bernard Shaw, P. G. Wodehouse, and Julian Huxley. A Mr. Armour-Milne complains in January of 1970:

> Three times in my life I have written a letter to the Editor. Three times he has found my letter interesting, but not sufficiently so to warrant publication. . . . What does one have to do in order to be recognized by the Editor of *The Times*?

At last with this letter Mr. Milne was published, and a few days later a Mr. Clark gives him a reply in the same section:

> It may be of interest to state that I have been privileged to have had over 40 letters published in *The Times*, and to indicate some of the subjects to which they referred: birds, animals, tomato plants, bats, caterpillars, hotels, the Christmas post, chemical sprays, railway closures, wintering in England, &c.

---

11. Kenneth Gregory, ed., *The First Cuckoo: A Selection of the Most Witty, Amusing and Memorable Letters to The Times, 1900–1980* (London: Allen and Unwin, 1981). There is now a *Second Cuckoo* (1983) and a *Third Cuckoo* (1985).—Trans.

During its brief history *El País* has received, as I mentioned, more than one hundred thousand letters and has published some four thousand. Obviously some kind of selection has to take place, and some readers show their understanding of this: "Whether this letter is published or not, I wish to compliment the publication of your newspaper, which though it will never be independent, is writing—or, better said, publishing—wonderful things."

Two hours a day of diversely shaded, human, sincere and passionate mail like this should not and cannot be disregarded. In early 1976 Jacques Fauvet, editor in chief of *Le Monde,* explained the success of his paper to me with these words:

> Our daily is austere in form and demanding to read, but we have dedicated ourselves to protesting and combating injustice. Blacks, the poor, the marginal, homosexuals, the handicapped, prisoners, and oppressed women find in us a forum for their voices.

Bound up in political and in semantic discussions of democracy, not a few leaders lose touch with the feelings and immediate concerns of the people. The political parties make public their long manifestos and programs in defense of legal conventions on abstract values. They often forget that among man's most primary needs and rights is to get social answers to the concrete problems of their coexistence. Spain is undergoing profound historic change. It is not only the regime of Franco that has disappeared, but also the entire vital, constitutional and constitutive conception of our existence as a nation. Catholicism, the keystone of national unity for the last five centuries, is no longer a political nexus, and indeed could no longer have been so. But this society, educated in the old manners and among old customs now being rapidly subverted—in the real and profound sense of that word—in its most traditional and unquestionably accepted values, needs something more than theoretical formulations on the value of freedom. The Spanish people are demanding a new scale of values, an imaginative horizon, different answers to different questions, and not a return to a nineteenth-century liberalism or to bourgeois formalities or social demagoguery. Our people have a history of freedom and compromise, which has been continually choked off by the structures of power. This tradition has a right to be reincarnated and to flourish.

The recent political change in this country has coincided with the most profound and moral generational changes experienced in this century. The problem is that when the society calls for a revolution in societal values, the powers that be offer only constitutional developments and expired formulas for generating out-of-date answers. The big question marks for the Spanish these days are not much different from those for the French, the Germans or the Italians; the questions are not really distinct from those facing our neighbors in Western Europe.

We have kept the dialogue for our time to a minimum. Europe, and Spain along with Europe, is suffering a crisis of imagination and leadership. It is not that the time of the great Buddhas has passed, it is rather that the little ones are going on in a permanent conspiracy that lets them subsist in the pinnacles of power. Our politicians need to get back in contact with the reality of the streets. They are caught up in their own intellectuality; they give sermons on praxis, but they don't actually practice what they preach.

After the ballot box, and I would say just about at the level of opinion polls, the daily papers are among the more revealing things around for those entrusted with the shaping of a community's moral and political behavior. For this reason, a little more reading of the sections of letters to the editor would go a long way in revealing the lives and problems facing the electorate. And it would help those leaders address some apparently insignificant questions, questions that themselves encompass a great question of our time: how is it possible to pull down the barriers to real communication and begin the common struggle for happiness?

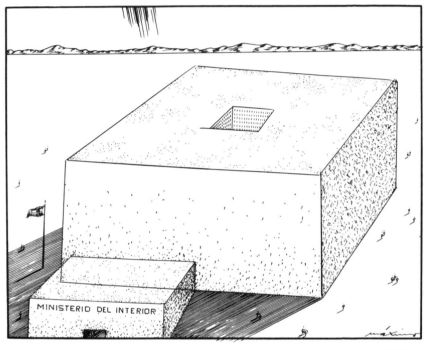

MINISTERIO DEL INTERIOR

El País

Chapter 5

Journalism and Politics

A recovery of the political nature of journalism, putting it back in touch with its most profound Hispanic heritage, has been needed for some time now. And more vividly than all others, the figure of the most exciting—-the adjective is an appropriate one—journalist of all times in our country, Mariano José de Larra,[1] stands as symbol of this tradition, as an example of what the Spanish press should not and cannot ever lose: critical sagacity and a permanent adversarial attitude toward power.

I have chosen to evoke Larra at the outset of this discussion because his words and ideas are so extraordinarily valid today that it seemed appropriate and even useful to do so. But the same thing could have been accomplished with Quevedo or Cervantes. I have always been amazed, for example, at how lightly the political imprisonment of Quev-

---

1. See note 5 in chapter 1.—TRANS.

edo by the Count Duke of Olivares is treated by our colleagues. I believe that if one sincerely wants to contribute to the spread of democracy and individual rights, he would do well to point out the central role freedom of speech has among the latter, and to remind all of how those who have defended or made use of it have been persecuted throughout Spanish history.

It is a common accusation, and one that I agree with, that on occasion journalists acquire excessive political influence, their words carrying inordinate weight among the political class. With good reason our newspapers have earned for themselves the appellation "paper parliament," a term that reflects the constant political debate carried on in their pages. During the last decade of the Franco regime, newspapers, by taking advantage of the small breach in the regime's structure of control afforded by the Fraga Law,[2] wore down the agonizing political institutions through tenacity and calculated risks, and made important contributions to the development of the great democratic debate that followed.

The actual advent of freedom, however, has shown us that this role as a paper parliament was not the specific result of circumstances created by the dictatorship. There was no reason for it to be so. From the beginnings of its existence journalism has had a right to be political. The history of the twentieth century is filled with examples—good and bad— of this, and without grasping this phenomenon one cannot understand the Spanish historical process of the last few centuries.

---

2. The Law of the Press of 1966. See also note 5 in the U.S. Preface.—TRANS.

Some will ask me how I can possibly combine this defense of the right of the journalist to be political with the acknowledgment of the criticism that on occasion journalists are excessively protagonistic in politics, and that the effect of their articles on public opinion is also excessive. Yet I do not see any necessary contradiction in this stance. The fact that journalism may be political does not mean that the figures of the journalist and the politician must be seen as indistinguishable. Above all, it is a good thing that they not be. A multitude of examples exist from both this and the last century of splendid professionals who, when they tried to combine the two specialties, found out that they were not made for both worlds. I will not succumb to the temptation of naming contemporary names, which are all too well known anyway; it will be enough to use Larra himself as an example of one who fell, in this case to the temptation of a seat in the Cortes from the hand of Istúriz. And he got it. He was sworn in on August 6, 1836, and six days later, as Professor Lomba y Pedraja said, he was "chopped to bits" by the insurgent sergeants of La Granja. This had a profound effect on Larra's subsequent prose, which in time became somber and brief, stripped of its former sparkle, and which was marked until his death by a steely cold edge.

In practically every respect, vices and errors included, Larra is paradigmatic of the Spanish political writer. My argument here does not concern the legitimacy of his political ambition, rather I assert his good luck. Would Larra the deputy have been so independent, daring and trenchant as Larra the journalist? And would he have remained as brilliant as he was after having lived with his contemporaries in power and after having assimilated the thousand and one excuses and themes comprising the logic of the state? Larra himself probably did not realize how thankful he as a literary figure should have been for the Granja insurrection and the loss of his seat. If he had not taken his own life so soon thereafter he would certainly have become aware of the dangers of his electoral adventure. After the event Larra was left without a seat, but we were left with his article "El día de los difuntos" (The day of the dead), the masterpiece of Spanish journalism of all time.[3]

A journalist who decided to cross the Rubicon and dedicate himself to matters of direct political action, as a member of government or representative of the opposition, is one who will probably never, even after abandoning that activity, be able to recover his status and credibility as an independent journalist. If he wants, he will be able to write partisan journalism or propaganda for his own ideas, but if he tries to write for a daily of liberal vocation it will be menaced through his simple presence with the stain of the color of the party he serves or served.

This all appears so logical, so tied to common sense, but nevertheless it is not so clearly so. If a person possesses large measures of both qualities he can be seen as a member of government or parliament and yet simultaneously take advantage of his professional status as a journalist. This often occurs in the Soviet Union, where the editor of a great newspaper is also of necessity a member of the politburo, and it also, of course, occurred under Francoism and in Hitler's Germany. We will now see how this can also occur in

---

3. I have not been able to find this article in translation. Readers who know Spanish may find it in Carlos Seco Serrano, ed., *Biblioteca de autores españoles*, Vol. 128 (Madrid: Atlas, 1960), 279–82.—Trans.

a country with a system of parliamentary democracy, by the grace and means of that mechanism that has come to receive the denomination "official license of journalist."

Journalism's Politicians

The propensity of journalists to be politicians is hardly censurable, however, if it is viewed in the light of a much worse tendency: that of politicians to become journalists. It is not much of a problem when whatever cabinet minister—or businessman, or playwright, or union leader—calls the newsroom to request that it not cover such and such because, among other things, *it is not news,* as they themselves have decided. Worse is when they call to ask that something be published because, among other things, *it is news,* and therefore deserves to be dressed in its professional and moral dignity even though it is nothing more than the product of a vulgar kind of pressure. But an even more curious custom has surfaced: deputies who keep their mouths shut on the floors of parliament out of party discipline and rules of order, then go out and write and write without stopping for the newspapers, and give uncountable press conferences or staged events. These people, embarked on political careers, evidently wish to limit their official action exclusively to the pushing of the voting button, and even in this simple action they foul up. This practice, inexplicably not cut off a long time ago, is helping to turn newspapers into a "paper parliament" in a somewhat more rigorous sense of the term. The press cannot publish the brilliant discourses and proposals the parliamentarians don't make, but the news desks are piled over with articles of moderate value and questionable prose by members of parliament. And we can just imagine what goes on down at the local papers, which have to deal with the heat from local bosses who have to justify their fiefdoms and favors without the aid of a seat in parliament.

This assault on the newsrooms by politicians, the striking example of intrusionism in our time, perverts the liberal and critical character of the press. Newspapers exist so that journalists may opine on the activities of politicians, but here the politicians usually offer the opinion articles while the journalists dedicate themselves to the conjuring of magical solutions to the politicians' problems. Such an inversion of roles almost always engenders press conferences in which one cannot quite tell, as the old saying goes, just who's doing the giving and who's doing the taking.

But why such a situation? Undoubtedly because the Spanish press, as we have said, has enormous influence among the political class. The custom of bringing down governments through the writing of articles is one of the purest in Spanish liberalism. "The Berenguer Error," an article by Ortega in the Madrid daily *El Sol* in which the famous subtitle *Delenda est Monarchia* was published, marked the end of a regime in much the same way as the famous gironazo of the spring of 1974 signaled the definitive collapse of Francoism in the midst of attempts at its liberalization—at least verbally—by poor inept Arias Navarro.[4]

---

4. "El Error Berenguer," *El Sol,* 15 November 1930. Ortega is the Spanish philosopher José Ortega y Gasset (1883–1955), author of a political essay, widely read in Anglo-American circles, called *The Revolt of the Masses* (New York: W.W. Norton, Co., 1957). Berenguer was General Dámaso Berenguer, who headed King

Felipe González *(center)*, head of the Spanish Socialist Workers Party and, since October, 1982, president of Spain. President González and his Defense Minister Narlis Serra *(far left)* visit the Brunete Armored Division Headquarters shortly after the 1982 elections, to celebrate the day of the patron saint of the Spanish Infantry. (Courtesy of *El País*.)

EL PAÍS

DIRECTOR: JUAN LUIS CEBRIAN   **DIARIO INDEPENDIENTE DE LA MAÑANA**   MADRID, VIERNES 29 DE OCTUBRE DE 1982

Redacción, Administración y Talleres: Miguel Yuste, 40 / Madrid-17 / ☏ 754 38 00 / Precio: 35 pesetas / Año VII. Número 2.044

EDICIÓN ESPECIAL DE LAS OCHO DE LA MAÑANA

Fraga será la oposición, con 105 diputados, mientras se hunden el centro y el Partido Comunista

El Partido Socialista, con 201 escaños, consigue la mayoría absoluta para gobernar la nación

La izquierda vuelve al poder en España, después de más de 43 años de Gobiernos de derechas, con el rotundo triunfo electoral del Partido Socialista Obrero Español (PSOE), que ayer consiguió, con 201 escaños, la mayoría absoluta en las terceras elecciones legislativas celebradas después de la muerte del general Franco, en 1975. La coalición de derechas integrada por Alianza Popular y el Partido Demócrata Popular (PDP) se convierte en la fuerza más importante de la oposición, con 105 diputados. El PSOE recibió el voto de más de 9.800.000 españoles (46%), frente a los 5.412.401 (25,3%) de Alianza Popular, según los resultados totales provisionales. El presidente del Gobierno, Leopoldo Calvo Sotelo, no obtuvo escaño. La jornada electoral estuvo dominada por una participación masiva, más del 79% del censo, y una absoluta normalidad.

El secretario general del PSOE y próximo presidente del Gobierno, Felipe González, abandona la tribuna desde la que esta madrugada se dirigió al pueblo español tras conocerse la abrumadora victoria electoral de su partido.   CHEMA CONESA

Felipe González Márquez, de cuarenta años de edad, que será con toda probabilidad el nuevo presidente del Gobierno español, afirmó esta madrugada, en su primera declaración al país tras la victoria, que "estamos preparados para llevar a cabo la responsabilidad que el pueblo español ha puesto en nuestras manos". El futuro primer ministro pidió el apoyo de todas las instituciones y de todos los sectores sociales para lograr el objetivo de "sacar España adelante".

Los electores decretaron ayer la práctica desaparición de la escena política de los partidos de centro, UCD (once diputados) y CDS (dos), así como del PCE, que sólo consiguió cinco diputados.

La jornada electoral y la celebración, en la madrugada, del triunfo socialista en las principales ciudades transcurrió con absoluta normalidad. En Madrid, miles de personas celebraron, en la calle Mayor y en la carrera de San Jerónimo, la victoria socialista. Un portavoz militar afirmó anoche que "el Ejército español respetará el resultado de las elecciones", y precisó que "la tranquilidad en el seno de las Fuerzas Armadas es total". El dirigente de la patronal, Carlos Ferrer, felicitó al PSOE y dijo que no teme a los socialistas en el poder, a pesar, precisó, del peligro de un aumento de la inflación y el paro.

El *sirón* socialista tuvo su reflejo en Euskadi y Cataluña, donde los socialistas superaron ampliamente anteriores resultados electorales y se convirtieron en la primera fuerza en Cataluña y en la segunda, muy próxima al PNV, en el País Vasco.

Convergència i Unió logró doce diputados y el PNV ocho. El nacionalismo de izquierda obtuvo tres diputados en el País Vasco: dos para Herri Batasuna y uno (dudoso) para Euskadiko Ezkerra. En Cataluña, Esquerra Republicana logró un escaño. El PSA y la extrema derecha desaparecen del Parlamento. Tejero obtuvo en todo el país 25.022 votos y Blas Piñar no renovó su escaño.

Manuel Fraga, líder de la alianza conservadora, manifestó su satisfacción por el resultado alcanzado, y afirmó que "se convertirá en una oposición eficaz al futuro Gobierno socialista". "Serviremos", añadió, "honestamente a la consolidación de la paz civil y al sistema constitucional".

Landelino Lavilla felicitó personalmente a Felipe González y manifestó que había habido "una respuesta a los estímulos de radicalización. Se demuestra que cuando el centro se desvía a la derecha se producen derrotas y decepciones".

El presidente del Gobierno garantizó que no habrá vacío de poder en el período que resta hasta la investidura del nuevo primer ministro.   **Páginas 14 a 28 y últimas**

El socialismo, en el poder

La victoria electoral del PSOE marca un hito histórico en el devenir político español. La presencia de ministros socialistas en los Gobiernos republicanos del primer bienio y de la etapa inmediatamente posterior al triunfo del Frente Popular no significó la asunción íntegra de sus responsabilidades del Estado por el PSOE. Aunque dos destacados dirigentes socialistas —Francisco Largo Caballero y Juan Negrín— ocuparon la presidencia del Consejo de Ministros durante la guerra civil, la atribulada historia de nuestro país durante esos tres años y las anormales condiciones del ejercicio del poder en plena contienda permiten afirmar que la victoria de Felipe González ofrece al partido que fundara Pablo Iglesias su primera oportunidad para dirigir la política española en situación de normalidad democrática.

Ha pasado mucho tiempo desde que aquel admirable luchador de las libertades pusiera la primera piedra de la organización que ayer obtuvo la victoria electoral. En muchas cosas el mundo, y nuestro país, es diferente. Son diferentes el propio nervio del socialismo en la Europa desarrollada y las relaciones internacionales heredadas de dos guerras mundiales sucesivas.

Pasa a la página 12

Partidos	% votos	Escaños	Escaños 1979
Censo: 26.837.212	Votantes: 21.353.996		Participación: 79,5%
Partido Socialista Obrero Español	46,00	201	121
Alianza Popular (AP-PDP)	25,30	105	9
Unión de Centro Democrático	7,20	11	168
Partido Comunista de España	3,80	5	23
Centro Democrático y Social	2,80	2	—
Convergència i Unió	3,70	12	8
Partido Nacionalista Vasco	1,51	8	7
Herri Batasuna	0,90	2	3
Euskadiko Ezkerra	0,40	1	1
Otros*	8,66	3	10

* Un diputado corresponde a Esquerra Republicana y los otros dos a la coalición AP-UCD en el País Vasco.

Front-page coverage of the 1982 electoral victory of the Spanish Socialist Workers Party and Felipe González *(center)* waving. (Courtesy of *El País*.)

EL PAIS

DIRECTOR: JUAN LUIS CEBRIAN   **DIARIO INDEPENDIENTE DE LA MAÑANA**   MADRID, MARTES 4 DE MAYO DE 1976

Redacción, Administración y Talleres: Miguel Yuste 38 / Madrid 17 / Teléfono 754 38 00 / Precio: 10 pesetas Sobretasa por transporte urgente: 1 peseta / Año 1, número 1.

Documento oficial del Parlamento Europeo sobre España

El reconocimiento de los partidos políticos, condición esencial para la integración en Europa

RAMON VILARO, **Bruselas**

La Comisión Política del Parlamento Europeo expresó su deseo de que España pueda incorporarse a las Comunidades Europeas «al término de una evolución hacia un régimen auténticamente democrático», según dicen en un comunicado oficial.

Dicho comunicado insiste en el restablecimiento de las libertades individuales, políticas y sindicales y, en particular, en la legalización de todos los partidos políticos, la amnistía y el regreso de los exiliados. «Medidas que deberían cotribuir a dar sentido a las *elecciones generales* anunciadas para la primavera de 1977.»

Dentro del ámbito de los contactos España-CEE destaca la visita de información a las Comunidades Europeas iniciada ayer por un grupo de 25 miembros del equipo de los cinco Partidos Democristianos del Estado español.

Los 25 miembros de la delegación democristiana española han sido oficialmente invitados en Bélgica por los partidos social-cristianos belgas, con objeto de informarles sobre el funcionamiento parlamentario y la preparación de elecciones municipales y generales.

Por otra parte, los ministros de Asuntos Exteriores de la CEE se encuentran reunidos en esta capital para una sesión de dos jornadas, a lo largo de las cuales definirán la postura común de los «Nueve» ante la Conferencia de las Naciones Unidas para la Cooperación (UNTACD); varios temas de política interior (como la elección por sufragio universal directo del Parlamento Europeo y el informe Tindemans sobre la «Unión Europea») y una serie de problemas de relaciones exteriores centrados en la demanda de adhesión de Grecia a la CEE, y la ayuda financiera de los «Nueve» a Portugal y a los países de la zona mediterránea que tienen acuerdos comerciales con la CEE.

Sir Cristopher Soames, vicepresidente de la Comisión Europea responsable de Relaciones Exteriores, informará oralmente el martes al Consejo de la CEE de los últimos contactos entre españoles y comunitarios —celebrados en Bruselas el 28 de abril— con vistas a la adaptación técnica del acuerdo comercial de 1970.

En la página 3, amplio informe de nuestro corresponsal en Bruselas sobre las relaciones de España con la Comunidad Económica Europea.

José María de Areilza   CIFRA

Guipúzcoa

Guardia civil muerto en un atentado

La población guipuzcoana de Legazpia fue escenario ayer de un doble atentado, a las cinco de la madrugada, un potente artefacto destrozaba el coche del regente del bar del frontón municipal. Ya de mañana, y en un viaje para dar cuenta del suceso anterior, resultó muerto el cabo primero de la Guardia Civil Antonio de Frutos Sualdes, que se dirigía en un coche hacia el cuartel desde el embalse Patricio Echevarría, donde se había colocado una *ikurriña* —bandera nacionalista vasca— conectada a una carga explosiva.

El vehículo quedó destrozado, y el cuerpo del guardia civil totalmente desfigurado.

Información en **pág. 13**

Areilza inicia mañana su visita a Marruecos

Mañana, miércoles, inicia su visita oficial a Marruecos el ministro de Asuntos Exteriores, José María de Areilza. La nueva correlación de fuerzas en el Magreb, tras la resolución del problema sahariano, y las "relaciones privilegiadas" que España y Marruecos mantienen desde el Tratado de Madrid, hace que el viaje del ministro español sea contemplado con interés y confianza.

Diversos problemas de envergadura serán abordados en el curso de esta visita: las expropiaciones de bienes españoles, el problema pesquero, las relaciones comerciales entre los dos países, la cuestión de los fosfatos de Bu—Craa y, probablemente, el contencioso territorial pendiente, es decir, Ceuta, Melilla y "los peñones".

El Sahara estará también presente en las conversaciones del señor Areilza con su colega marroquí.

Información en **pág. 8**

Ante la "reforma"

Coincide la aparición primera de EL PAIS con momentos singulares de la convivencia española. Desde la muerte del general Franco, y quizá antes, desde el asesinato del presidente Carrero, nuestro pueblo permanece en una constante y prolongada expectativa de cambio político que no acaba de producirse. Cuantos experimentos se han hecho desde el poder en los últimos dos años para tratar de asumir las profundas transformaciones operadas entre los españoles e integrarlas en el régimen vigente han fracasado.

La incuestionable reformista que el Rey asumiera en los tempranos días de su llegada al Trono parece condenada a similar destino, dada la actitud del gabinete ministerial. La pérdida de credibilidad de la política gubernamental es, con términos, definitiva. Y ni el reciente discurso del presidente Arias ni las promesas, siempre incumplidas, de democratización consiguen ya prender en la esperanza de los españoles.

No es cuestión de impaciencia. Este país lleva esperando cuarenta años —exactamente desde el comienzo de la guerra civil— la normalización de su convivencia política. Este país, cuyas tres cuartas partes de la población no participaron en aquella contienda fratricida, busca intúilmente, por lo mismo, desde hace casi medio siglo unas formas de vida civilizadas y modernas que le permitan encontrar en el concierto de las naciones el lugar que por historia y por derecho le pertenece. Y la espera contenida del pasado, preñada de ilusiones cuando se pensaba en fechas como las que ahora vivimos, se ha visto repetidamente defraudada.

En este primer número de un periódico que nace al amparo de una convicción irrenunciablemente democrática, hay que decir que la reforma política anunciada ni satisface las exigencias mínimas que el respeto a los principios de la democracia y de la libertad exigen, ni puede lograr la adhesión de las nuevas generaciones de españoles.

El *reformismo* del poder ha naufragado porque no ha sido sincero. En una palabra: no ha sido verdadera y realmente reformista. Las esperanzas de un tránsito lineal entre la dictadura de antaño y un sistema democrático han sido siempre pocas; resultaban no obstante plausibles por el dato de que los pueblos, repetidas veces demostrado, de encontrar soluciones a una situación sin salida como la provocada por el antiguo régimen. Pero para que la dialéctica de la reforma hubiera podido anular con convicción a la dialéctica de la ruptura, tenía que haber comenzado por el reconocimiento de que las metas de una y otra tienen que ser en cualquier caso parejas: la instauración de una democracia real en nuestro suelo, con el reconocimiento de las libertades individuales y del derecho de los ciudadanos a elegir a sus gobernantes a través del sufragio universal. La *reforma* que el Go-

bierno quiere vender hoy a la opinión viene sólo a defender privilegios e intereses de grupo que nos hablan de la continuidad de un pasado sin horizontes.

Quizá todavía sería hoy posible una estrategia de reforma, a condición de que fuera otro gobierno el que la emprendiera y tuviera credibilidad entre los ciudadanos. De otro modo, cuando el Presidente anuncie calendarios y programas parecerá que esdibuye su turno ordenado para cometer errores inútiles. No es un prejuicio esto que decimos. Las líneas conocidas de las leyes políticas enviadas a las Cortes hacen subsistir el antiguo aparato burocrático y político del Régimen y del Movimiento bajo la capa medrosa de un nombre venerable, el de Senado; solución esta que no solucionada nada y no satisface a nadie. La existencia de una Cámara Alta con facultades colegislativas de hecho superiores a las de la Baja —elegida por sufragio universal— y con funciones similares al actual Consejo Nacional en lo que respecta a la salvaguarda de las LeyesFundamentales; la permanencia de los cuarenta consejeros de Ayete —designados por Franco— con carácter vitalicio; la de unos senadores elegidos por representación sindical, con la ambigüedad que su.po-ne el elegir tal cosa sin que se tenga noticia previa de cómo va a articularse la propia reforma de nuestros sindicatos; y la existencia final de un Comité de Vigilancia del Senado con notable presencia de senadores de designación franquista y con altas atribuciones sobre todo, el cuerpo legislativo, son ejemplos de que las «soluciones» del gobierno Arias están teñidas de caetanismo y, por tanto, de inutilidad cara a un futuro no lejano. Si añadimos a ello que existe una propuesta para que los principios Fundamentales del Movimiento no sean reformables ni a través del Referéndum, que el antiguo Secretario General del Partido permanece en el gabinete bajo la denominación de Ministro Secretario General del Gobierno, y que finalmente este no es responsable de nada ante una Cámara Baja elegida por sufragio universal —que lógicamente es quien debe representar la voluntad de los ciudadanos— podrá entenderse hasta qué punto la *reforma* está condenada al fracaso. Porque no ha consentido en una verdadera reforma. Pero amenaza además con arrastrar en su caída a toda otra posibilidad de reformismo auténtico que pudiera haber contado con un asentimiento generalizado.

Y esto es cuanto queríamos decir en nuestro primer día de existencia. Si como saludo resulta intemperante, acéptese al menos como inicial impresión de un diario recién nacido que, apenas abre los ojos y mira en torno suyo, no tiene otro remedio que pronunciar de nuevo las palabras de Ortega, tan entrañables para nosotros: Desde luego, señores *«no es esto, no es esto».*

Información sobre la reforma parlamentaria en **pág. 11**

King Juan Carlos receives the principal political party leaders on October 27, 1982, the eve of national elections. The King offers an ashtray to inveterate smoker Santiago Carrillo, then head of the Spanish Communist Party. (Courtesy of *El País*.)

President Adolfo Suárez *(far right)* in a solemn, pensive moment in 1979. The photographer's composition had prophetic elements: Suárez would resign within two years. (Courtesy of *El País*.)

EL PAIS

DIRECTOR: JUAN LUIS CEBRIAN · DIARIO INDEPENDIENTE DE LA MAÑANA · MADRID, MARTES 24 DE FEBRERO DE 1981

Redacción, Administración y Talleres: Miguel Yuste, 40. Madrid-17 / Teléfono 754 38 00 / Precio: 25 pesetas / Año VI. Número 1.494

EDICION DE LAS DOS DE LA MADRUGADA

El general Milans del Bosch retiró las tropas de las calles
de Valencia tras el mensaje del Rey

El intento de golpe de Estado, en vías de fracaso

El golpe de Estado protagonizado ayer tarde por un destacamento compuesto por 150 guardias civiles al mando del teniente coronel Tejero —conspirador de la *operación Galaxia*— parece en vías de fracaso. Pese a la tensión del momento —el Gobierno y el Parlamento permanecen como rehenes de los rebeldes en el palacio del Congreso—, la situación era normal en todo el país, salvo en Valencia, donde el general Milans del Bosch decretó por su cuenta el

toque de queda, tomó la ciudad bajo su exclusiva autoridad y desplegó fuerzas acorazadas y mecanizadas en los puntos estratégicos. La ciudad estaba prácticamente en manos militares, pero el capitán general dio orden de retirar las tropas tras el mensaje por televisión del Rey. El Rey se puso en contacto con la Junta de Jefes de Estado Mayor e indicó a los subsecretarios y secretarios de Estado que se constituyeran en Gabinete para contrarrestar la intentona de los rebel-

des, que mantenían como rehenes al Gobierno de la nación y a todos los parlamentarios. Fuerzas leales a la autoridad constitucional, compuestas por efectivos de la Policía Nacional, GEO y Guardia Civil, rodeaban a medianoche el edificio del Parlamento y conminaron a los sublevados para que depusieran su actitud. Don Juan Carlos se dirigió a todos los ciudadanos por RTVE. Los diputados votaban la investidura de Calvo Sotelo cuando los rebeldes irrumpieron en el

hemiciclo e interrumpieron la normalidad constitucional.   **Páginas 11 a 21 y última**

Lacónico mensaje del Rey

"La Corona defiende la Constitución"

Página 10

El teniente coronel Tejero, conspirador de la *operación Galaxia*, al mando de un grupo de rebeldes, ocupa el palacio del Congreso de los Diputados, y desde el atril de oradores conmina a los parlamentarios, pistola en mano, mientras que otros guardias civiles les encañonan con sus fusiles automáticos y les obligan a tenderse en el suelo bajo sus escaños.

Guardias civiles rebeldes se hacen fuertes en el Congreso y mantienen como rehenes al Gobierno y al Parlamento

Front-page coverage of the coup attempt of February 23, 1981. (Courtesy of *El País*.)

EL PAIS

DIRECTOR: JUAN LUIS CEBRIÁN
DIARIO INDEPENDIENTE DE LA MAÑANA
MADRID, VIERNES 31 DE ENERO DE 1986
Redacción, Administración y Talleres: Miguel Yuste, 40 / 28037 Madrid / ☎ (91) 754 38 00 / Precio: 60 pesetas / Año XI. Número 3.223

MARISA FLÓREZ

El Príncipe de Asturias saluda al Rey, tras jurar la Constitución, en presencia de su abuelo, don Juan de Borbón; las infantas, Cristina y Elena; el presidente del Gobierno, Felipe González, y la Reina. De espaldas, el presidente del Congreso, Gregorio Peces-Barba.

Las Cortes y el Gobierno, testigos del acatamiento de la Constitución por el Príncipe

La jura de Felipe de Borbón subraya la continuidad democrática de la Monarquía

El príncipe de Asturias, Felipe de Borbón y Grecia, juró ayer "guardar y hacer guardar la Constitución", así como fidelidad al Rey, el mismo día en que alcanzaba la mayoría de edad, en una sesión solemne de las Cortes, reunidas en el palacio del Congreso. La continuidad de la institución de la Corona a partir de las

El presidente del Congreso, Gregorio Peces-Barba, en su discurso en las Cortes definió la monarquía parlamentaria como la forma política del Estado "más adecuada y racional" para esta época. Más tarde, en el palacio de Oriente, el presidente del Gobierno, Felipe

exigencias constitucionales se materializó en una solemne ceremonia ante el Gobierno en pleno. A sistieron al acto diputados y senadores, familia real, cuerpo diplomático, presidentes de las comunidades autónomas y representantes de las altas instituciones del Estado.

González, y el Príncipe de Asturias pronunciaron unas palabras que recibió la condecoración y pronunció unas palabras con las que no el collar de la Real Orden de Carlos III.

Los actos se desarrollaron en dos ceremonias distintas, la primera en el Congreso y la segunda

en el palacio Real, donde el Príncipe recibió la condecoración y pronunció unas palabras en las que destacó la adhesión del presidente y del Gobierno a la institución encarnada en su persona como sucesor.

Felipe González, en un breve

parlamento, afirmó, entre otras cosas, que "esta España democrática y libre apuesta hoy por su futuro constitucional en la persona de vuestra alteza real".

La recepción en el palacio de Oriente congregó a cerca de un millar de invitados, en representación de estamentos profesionales, sociales y culturales, así como también a los miembros del jurado internacional que hoy fallará en Oviedo el primer premio Príncipe de Asturias a la libertad.

Páginas 13 a 15

Páginas 13 a 15

Un temporal bate la costa malagueña y caen grandes nevadas en el Norte

Un fuerte temporal de poniente batió ayer la costa meridional del Mediterráneo. Dos marineros, uno de nacionalidad española y otro marroquí, se ahogaron en el naufragio del carguero español *Alpro*, hundido a tres millas de la costa malagueña por un desplazamiento de su carga de caolín. Cinco personas más, que viajaban a bordo, figuran como desaparecidas. En Arenys de Mar (Barcelona) se ahogó un pescador.

El temporal provocó un oleaje con olas de cinco a siete metros y obligó a cerrar el puerto de Ceuta. Los aviones que enlazan Málaga

con Melilla no pudieron despegar. Al mismo tiempo, intensas nevadas cayeron en Galicia, Asturias, León, Cantabria y Cataluña, donde faltó la luz en casi la mitad de la región. Numerosos pueblos de la cordillera Cantábrica quedaron incomunicados. A primera hora de la madrugada de hoy se cerró la carretera de Burgos en el kilómetro 77, en Buitrago. Varios puertos de la sierra madrileña también estaban cerrados y se necesitaban cadenas en los de Navacerrada y Los Leones, así como en tramos de la carretera de La Coruña. **Páginas 20 y 30**

Hoy se conocerán la pregunta y el día del referéndum sobre la OTAN

El Gobierno acordará hoy el decreto de convocatoria del referéndum sobre la permanencia de España en la OTAN, y lo enviará este mediodía a las Cortes, así como el preceptivo comunicado previo al debate sobre seguridad exterior, que comenzará el próximo martes.

Todas las fuentes socialistas y gubernamentales consultadas por este periódico admitieron como fecha más probable para la celebración del referéndum la del miércoles 12 de marzo. También señalaron que lo más probable es que la

pregunta solicite el apoyo a la decisión del Gobierno de permanecer en la Alianza con los condicionantes conocidos de la no integración en el mando militar, la no nuclearización de España y la reducción de los efectivos militares norteamericanos en el país.

Por otra parte, el sindicato socialista UGT anunció ayer que mantendría su voto contra la permanencia de España en la OTAN, al tiempo que acordaba no autorizar a sus dirigentes a hacer campaña a favor de la citada permanencia. **Página 17**

The front-page photo on January 31, 1986, shows the Prince of Asturias taking an oath of loyalty to the Spanish Constitution in the presence of the Spanish royal family and President Felipe González. The accompanying story notes the significance of this event for democratic continuity in Spain. (Courtesy of *El País*.)

Secretary of State for Relations with the Common Market Manuel Marin during a break in the 1985 negotiating sessions in Brussels. The entry of Spain into the European Economic Community, a singularly important event in Spanish history, nevertheless unfolds very slowly. (Courtesy of *El País*.)

From my point of view, the absence of a real public opinion in our country weakens the claim of representation made by our democratic administrations. It is not easy to understand how a press with low circulation and even lower readership, estimated at 20 to 25 percent of all voters, can be so powerful. It becomes more understandable, however, when one accepts the notion that the elite and the opinion leaders influence voter decisions or political judgments almost solely on the basis of articles read in the papers. Even more surprising, in a country as enthusiastic for autonomy as ours is, the provincial reader avidly follows stories in the Madrid papers and maintains surprising and admirable loyalty to them. In today's Spain it is still easy to see the local doctor, pharmacist and intellectual getting together in their daily discussions and sharing with each other the doctrines and counsel offered in such and such newspaper from the capital. The opinions expressed in the

Alfonso XIII's government for fifteen months after the previous dictator, Miguel Primo de Rivera, lost his bases of support and went into exile after ruling Spain for seven years. Berenguer left power in 1931, the same year in which Alfonso XIII abdicated the throne and went into exile. The term *gironazo* is explained in chapter 4, note 7. Carlos Arias Navarro was the last president of the government under Franco and, by default, the first president under King Juan Carlos. He was overwhelmed by the pull of two opposing forces. The old Francoist guard hurled gironazos at him while from the other side the vast popular hunger for political and social change—well voiced in the newspapers—made his attempts at change appear slow and inept. He could not decide which way to go, and he resigned shortly after some very uncomplimentary statements about him, attributed to Juan Carlos and published in *Newsweek*, were not denied by the king. See Raymond Carr and Juan Pablo Fusi, *Spain: Dictatorship to Democracy* (London: Allen and Unwin, 1979), 195–217. Miguel Primo de Rivera and his son José Antonio are discussed in a later note, though another father-son combination should be mentioned here. The man most responsible for organizing the financial structure of *El País* and for finding backers for the project in the early 1970s was Jesús Ortega, son of the Spanish philosopher José Ortega y Gasset.—TRANS.

latter will affect the local residents in unseen ways, as they are accustomed to listening to and heeding the advice of these "local wise ones."

In the final analysis, nonetheless, newspapers are nothing more than newspapers, and journalists nothing else but a means of connection between events and readers, between reality and analysis. In spite of this they are asked to be, like the famous "Joseantonian Man,"[5] half-monk and half-soldier: miserably paid but incorruptible, poorly educated yet omniscient, socially mistreated yet admired, generous, feared. . . . What race of men would resist the volume of corruption, social favors, cynicism and manipulation that rains down on journalists from the ruling classes? What race of animals wouldn't feel a sense of repugnance at the veneration provoked in our country for simple hackwork, be it for the right or the left? All of those reasons mentioned previously combined with a certain reigning theory on the world of information have led the political class to expound loudly and at length on the responsibilities of the press and

5. Miguel Primo de Rivera ruled Spain under King Alfonso XIII in a kind of benevolent dictatorial fashion from 1923 to 1930. Over time both he and his government acquired a rather unsavory hedonistic image, which contributed to his downfall. One of his sons, José Antonio Primo de Rivera seemed to pick up on this frame of iniquity. José Antonio became a leader of the Spanish National Socialist Movement and a cofounder of the Spanish Falange in the 1930s. He was a charismatic speaker and his speeches were knit together with a strong thread of ascetic moralism—one should be pure, be strong, be Spanish and fight for the unity of a pure and sacred Spain, resisting secular temptations that were eating away at the national moral fabric. There seems to be a logical gap here: Cebrián begins by evoking an image of ascetic state worship and then moves on to the more familiar grounds of journalistic ethics. The gap is a difficult one concerning the nature of fascism, and those readers interested in learning more about the Spanish variety might wish to read Stanley Payne, *Falange: History of Spanish Fascism* (Palo Alto: Stanford University Press, 1965).—TRANS.

of journalists. Following closely behind their expositions is usually punishment. Every time I hear such a sermon I begin to tremble. Responsible journalists? Sure. The same as responsible bankers, responsible politicians, responsible military leaders, responsible businessmen, architects, doctors, diplomats, police. . . . But in the judgment of our political class just what is an *irresponsible journalist?* Is he one who misquotes, lies, or accepts payoffs? No. He is just the one who misquotes those in power—not those who slander the opposition. Only he who accepts a check that is not official, one that does not come from slush funds, from administration officials, or for services rendered to the grand and sacred monster of the state.

It appears that there are just two classes of journalists in Spain, because to infer from those who demand "responsibility" so much and so haughtily, either there are no honest ones or their number is too small to count. Hence, there are journalists who are paid by those in power and journalists who are paid by Moscow. Those who are paid by power are responsible. Those who aren't—all the others—are therefore on the Moscow payroll. One more detail to keep in mind: in every case the "irresponsible one," socially speaking, is the subsidized journalist and not the minister or hierarchy doing the subsidizing. Knowing how to utilize slush funds is a mark of distinction in our political class, not a misdeed.

In reality, what are politicians seeking when they request responsible journalists? They are demanding journalists without independence, fearful and limp. Journalists who are not journalists, who don't write anything unless it is in dictation, and even then not a whole lot of that. If they followed the line set down by the powerful—not just in government, but also the de facto powers (as they have come to be called) that have surrounded and inundated us forever, it seems—if journalists follow those lines as the powerful would have them, then it would have to be concluded that neither Cervantes nor Quevedo nor Lope nor Jovellanos nor Larra nor Ganivet nor many others would have made it to the annals of Spanish literature. Neither Cela nor Umbral would have written any of their best prose. But, of course, they would have been very responsible. They wouldn't attack, wouldn't hurt or bother anyone, wouldn't—pardon the expression—screw their fellow man. They would have been made public relations managers for some corporation, university, or even trade union. They would carry press cards with all the appropriate validations. And, of course, newspapers wouldn't have come into being either because no one would have read them.

We have talked about Larra. The censorship in his day tried—as it always does—to make journalists responsible. Once again the state wished to educate, protect, and safeguard. It is spine-chilling to note how in such different historical circumstances a century and a half later, the prose of Figaro[6] on these questions not only continues to be modern in its literary dimension, but also in its complaints and denunciations.

And all of this should and must be said at a moment when we are threatened—I repeat threatened—with a Law of Information, which under the pretext of establishing regulations and order I fear is up to nothing more than the resurrection of old walls and obstacles to the freedom of

---

6. A pen name of Mariano Jose de Larra.—TRANS.

expression. A democratic country does not need any kind of specific legislation for the press. Ordinary law is sufficient to establish the socially appropriate control. A liberal—in the broadest and noblest sense of the word—conception of freedom of the press goes against any kind of normative legislation that tries to limit it, and instead moves toward a system of self-control through systems such as press councils, with the effective participation of readers in that control.

The concept of journalistic responsibility as the political class usually understands it, nevertheless, is one that would lead to the extinction of the species. I certainly want to see responsible journalists: informed, writing well, courageous of pen and heart. I don't want them to be monks or soldiers but critical and disobedient of the society they serve.

I want to see, once and for all, newsrooms populated with journalists and not with bureaucrats, newsrooms filled with creators, experts, and even dreamers. Everything that a member of parliament these days is not. Only then will newspapers be able to perform their function as society's designated adversaries, checking abuses and exposing corruption.

What is the reality of the situation if we stop and look at it today? The reality is that newspapers rarely and decreasingly exercise this function. They are being integrated, chewed up and smoothly digested by the mouthpieces of the new political class. The same is true for the government as for the opposition.[7] Weighed down with the historic task of

---

7. At the time this essay was written, Adolfo Suárez of the Democratic Center Union Party formed the government while the opposition included, in order of voting power, the socialists of Felipe González, the conservatives of Manuel Fraga Ibarne,

promoting consensus, reducing tensions, escaping from threats of coups d'etat, newspapers lower their sights, adjust themselves to the general need, the common good, to the service of the country. Almost exclusively it is the journalist of the extreme right who sharpens his pencil and tries to construct an opposition press. But that's like the saying that from the sublime to the ridiculous there is just one short step, because there is barely the same distance between honest criticism and libel. Using democracy to destroy it, and making use of freedom to bring it to an end is anything but a respectable posture. And those gentlemen who pay for, read and write in that press are precisely the same ones who some years before swamped us, as they still do today, with their diatribes on the sincerity of the Spanish being! The press and journalists of the extreme right are not trying to intervene in politics, they are trying to terminate any political activity that is not their own. And from Lenin they learned two of the maxims they go by. The first is that the journalist is the best political agitator—and they do dedicate themselves to agitation. The second is the one that ponders the ends of liberty. They would rather talk about its origins than about the concept itself.

The political class, we were saying, has launched an all-out assault on the newsrooms. This is how what Balzac, that great contemporary of Larra, called the politician of the newspaper is born. "Every newspaper has," he says,

> not counting its publisher, editor in chief, its compositor of filler articles, or its behind-the-scenes shakers and supporters, in

---

and then, with roughly equal power, the Catalonian and Basque regionalist parties, and the Spanish Communist Party.—TRANS.

addition, a man who gives it its color, its unity, a man who ostensibly or mutely protects it. People come to say of him: "He's a political man." A political man is one who is firmly connected to power, or who is going to be, or who once enjoyed these connections and wishes to do so again. At times he's a myth: he doesn't exist, or else he doesn't have an idea in his head.

"The newspaper," Balzac adds,

> is the newspaper, and the political man its prophet. These prophets are more prophetic for what they do not say than for what they do. No one is more infallible than a mute prophet.

From which the French writer extracts this axiom: "The more empty-headed the politician, the more likely it is that he will become the Grand Lama of a newspaper."[8]

Spain has more than its share of grand lamas and pseudosaints in the press and in practically everything else too. But the function of the press is to defrock pseudosaints. It takes very little effort to name these Buddhas of literature and politics who move through the newsrooms as if they were the all-stars of opinion. The right is plagued with them, and the left has no other ambition than to achieve their status. Ministers and leaders are dying to write editorials; they aren't satisfied with merely dictating decrees. To paraphrase Javier Pradera, they have the power and now they want the glory, too. It's just too much.

Is it possible to find a line, a modus operandi, which at

---

8. Excerpts translated from Balzac's *Monographie de la Press Parisienne* (Paris: Aubry, 1943). I cannot locate an English translation of this work.—TRANS.

the same time can save newspapers from being swallowed up by the powerful or ruined through disputes with them? There should be. But it demands an honest and imaginative effort by those dedicated to the range of informative activities. Above all it demands an effort by journalists to clarify their position and actions within the political and social structure. How can this be done when almost half the profession is employed—some journalists have two, three, and even four separate jobs—by the state? How can we expect journalists of the apparatus to be adversaries of the apparatus? This question of the machinery of power, adhered to and venerated by the political class, in the words of ex-minister Garrigues,[9] like a fountain of wealth, should be contemplated by the mass media in its proper dimension. Ex-minister Garrigues, for example, since we've brought him up, accuses the ship of state of devouring everything, but he himself got aboard ship every chance he could. After all, isn't it the dream of just about any Spaniard to have a civil servant's salary? In this, journalists are no different; there is too much love for official limousines among my colleagues. An official limousine may be the symbol of having achieved power, the power of the apparatus. I will keep my independence.

I and many others. The recovery of this independent role requires the disappearance of certain traps and obstacles to

---

9. Antonio Garrigues y Díaz Canabate, professor of law and author of a much-used text on business law, was a civil servant in Franco's government during and after the Spanish Civil War, ambassador to the United States during the Kennedy years, ambassador to the Vatican after that, and minister of justice during the first government of Juan Carlos. Cebrián frames this Spanish proponent of laissez faire liberalism somewhat ironically.—TRANS.

informative activity. The first of these to go should be the requirement that journalists be licensed, something promoted and demanded, incredibly, by the Federation of Spanish Press Associations itself. A liberal conception of the press—and the history of freedom of the press is inextricably tied to constitutional liberalism—demands just the opposite. As the English Press Council defines it, the right to freedom of information means that every citizen has the right to walk down the street, stop, look around and relate what he sees to others. The right is not solely for journalists but for the entire society. Journalists are just its administrators for their readers and listeners. This conception of the freedom of information as a public right should be learned well by our press impresarios, for example. While they are, of course, the owners of newspapers, they do not own either the news they publish or the public's right to know the news. Those in government—who in many cases are also businessmen—should learn this too, and so should many press professionals, who not infrequently seem to be out to confuse themselves with those in government, or at least with their court jesters.

How can one reconcile the vision of a pluralistic and open practice of journalism with a solitary means of access to it? The two are irreconcilable. Journalists should be anything but a caste. We have protested so much over the existence of closed and secret organizations in our society, and now we want to create one of our own. To know how to make the practice of journalism possible, but guaranteeing adequate education for future professionals without administrative red tape and without creating a new class of experts in nothing, which now threatens to fill our newsrooms, is a challenge for the press worldwide. Pretending to solve this problem by issuing licenses is to evade both the challenge and reality itself. But we Spaniards are experts at passing laws that do not have to be obeyed. And in the end, we will have a law of information and official licensing and neither will accomplish anything.

The press has no need for licensing. It needs instead a great internal remodeling, a major move toward modern investigative practices, which will return to it the credibility and support of its readers. When the crisis or the press is discussed, and it is a reality born of many factors—narrowness of market, nonexistence of commercial channels, increasing costs of raw materials, and more—too often the real crisis of content of our newspapers is overlooked. The initial wave of yellow journalism practiced by some publications in the first years of the political transition has filled the pages of newspapers with scandals no one believes and accusations nobody notices. Nevertheless, the national scandals, corruption, and agitation are out there. We have already seen how power in all its manifestations strives to bribe journalists—and bribes are not made with just money. A bribe is a logical stance for those in power who fear controls and denunciations by the press (a true challenger of power in its most desirable version). But without seeking to embark on a crusade, journalists should understand that it is their mission to lift up the rug a little so that the dirt underneath can be seen. To do this, clearly, one must have one's own house in order.

This has been a personal and almost intimate sojourn through the problems that an editor, impassioned with an almost platonic love of politics, has to deal with concerning the relationship that the press and politics maintain with each other in democratic Spain. Much more remains to be written, as, for example, on the constitutional issues of the conscience clause and professional secrecy, on the status of television and radio, on the role of the autonomous communities with respect to the mass media, and on the explication of the role of the press as transforming agent in social and political reality, a role that was so visible in the last years of Francoism and the first years of the democracy. But I have thought it best for now to render this minimal homage to Larra, to show what is sorely missing among today's professionals. The picture he ultimately painted of early nineteenth century Spain remains so clearly alive that we could well ask ourselves just what the politicians, intellectuals, social leaders, and journalists have been doing all this while. In spite of our finding ourselves in the midst of a microelectronic era, in a century of atomic energy and television, we continue to launch high into the stratosphere, with great fanfare and publicity in the newspapers and other media, what Larra described as "balloon-men":

> . . . look at the balloon-man with all his characteristics. What noise beforehand! "The ascent! He's going to get in! Now he's just about to climb in!" Great fame, great prestige. Their balloon is readied for them; they're entrusted with it; look how they swell up! Who can doubt their ability. But like almost all our balloons, while they're down among us their greatness, preparation, and fame cause wonderment; but as they climb they begin to look smaller. When he's as high as the Palace, which in truth is not very high, he looks as small as a hazelnut; the balloon-man is nothing by now: a bit of smoky air; a large sheet,

empty and blank. And of course, once up, there's no direction. Is it possible that no one can find a way to direct and steer this balloon?[10]

Without a doubt there are too many balloon-men in this country. Our firmament is peppered with them, and as Balzac would have said, the fewer ideas they have, the higher they rise.

Hence, spiking balloons is a worthy proposition for today's press, although some illustrious personage may burst, and not with self-satisfaction. This does not weaken democracy, it consolidates it, and it helps create what we have not yet created in Spain: true freedom. Through our review of these two great authors, Larra and Balzac—or Balzac and Larra—we may conclude that yes, liberties do, of course, exist in Spain, liberties of all sorts, but not freedom.

---

10. The original may be found in Carlos Seco Serrano, *Biblioteca de autores españoles,* vol. 128 (Madrid: Atlas, 1960). The translation offered here is essentially that of Pierre Ullman, *Mariano de Larra and Spanish Political Rhetoric* (Madison, Wisconsin: University of Wisconsin Press, 1971), 361–62. I have made some minor modifications of the Ullman text.—TRANS.

PAUL CÉZANNE

El País

Chapter 6

How the Public Receives the News

In Minneapolis, Minnesota, in 1962 there was a prolonged newspaper strike. The *Star* and the *Tribune,* the only dailies in the city, had closed down for labor reasons. The inhabitants of Minneapolis hence began to pay more attention than normal to radio and television news broadcasts and to buy more magazines and newsweeklies than usual. Petty thieves scurried off to the sister city of St. Paul to steal papers from the street vending machines and later sell them on the black market in the city without a press. But as the strike continued, an advertising agent came up with the idea of making an agreement with a printer, contracting a group of reporters, establishing an improvised distribution system, and founding a newspaper that, obviously, did not use the wire services. Without much imagination he baptized it *The Daily Herald* and in a few days he had its circulation up over 100,000 copies a day.

This anecdote was related to us by William Rivers, maestro of American journalism,[1] and it could very well lay to rest certain notions about the survivability of the newspaper in the face of other mass media. I believe it an appropriate prologue to an issue so mundane in appearance that we rarely pause to take note of it: how the public receives the news.

Do the electronic media threaten the print media? Are we slowly but inexorably approaching the phantasmagorical world of *Fahrenheit 451,* and through it a social unification of culture and ideas? Does television permit equal and even greater possibilities for the cultural and mental development of society than did the book and the newspaper? And does it respect the canons of freedom that are so essential to the configuration of democratic life?

In the less developed countries, where a large part of the population—at times approaching 60 and 70 percent—is illiterate, television is the mass medium through which news, as we traditionally understand it, can be broadcast. There are hundreds of millions of people in these countries who are dependent to unimaginable extremes on this marvelous little box, which in more literate societies has come to be known almost unanimously as the *idiot box.*

However, a new and disconcerting fact is beginning to superimpose itself on traditional culture, even in industrialized communities. Before learning to read, children have received such a volume of knowledge from the small screen that they know many more things about the world than

---

1. The story is related in Rivers's text, *Mass Media* (New York: Harper and Row, 1962).—Trans.

many of their predecessors could have learned in a lifetime of reading.

In the first place, all of these things should lead us to appreciate the value of television as a medium for the diffusion of culture. Whatever the criticism raised over its ultimate effects, and for intellectuals this is great sport, the formidable benefits that television, in this regard, can bring to humanity should be the starting point for discussion.

According to a 1977 survey for RTVE,[2] 93 percent of all Spaniards have television sets and 81 percent habitually watch prime-time programming. This means that between ten and eleven at night, approximately fourteen million Spaniards are concentrated in front of their sets, one of the largest imaginable audiences for any European or Western television network. From this we can calculate that over twelve million people watch the evening news broadcast. For the majority of them TVE is the only means of information they have, and it is estimated that 65 percent of the population receive their news first on television. Only a small portion of them go on later to the newspapers and magazines to augment their information.

A working Spaniard over thirty years of age will spend an average of two hours a day in front of the television, and will not spend more than ten or fifteen minutes reading a newspaper. But we should not be misled by the manipulation of statistics; barely 17 percent of this category of Spaniards (the most significant and influential group in society) habitually read the newspapers.

---

2. Radio y Televisión Española (TVE), the state media corporation.—TRANS.

Not only among Spaniards has this been a cause for concern. Chancellor Helmut Schmidt went to the length of proposing that Germans give up television at least one day a week. Keeping in mind that in the Federal Republic of Germany the average citizen is in front of the television four and a half hours a day (figure from the *Cultural and Political Review* of Frankfurt), one will understand the chancellor's proposal and also the following comment made by the bishop of Hamburg: "Human liberation from television should commence posthaste."

But the bishop exaggerates, undoubtedly out of his condition as a cleric. Other statistics and considerations lend a less pejorative shading to the assessment television deserves as a means of social communication. The first medium for the communication of news in the United States continues to be the newspaper (69 percent), followed by television (62 percent), and then radio (49 percent). Only 25 percent of all Americans habitually use all three media and the vast majority confess that they have received the basic information they need by midday. Here then is evidence of how the "idiot box" has not overshadowed other possibilities of cultural and journalistic development in the world's most developed society. When James Reston said in the *New York Times* that if the nineteenth century was the heyday for novelists, the twentieth century is so for journalists, he was not lacking in support for that assertion.[3]

Hundreds of scientific and sociological studies, surveys,

<hr />

3. This thesis is also discussed in William Rivers, *The Opinion Makers* (Boston: Beacon Press, 1965). The figures on U.S. mass media usage cited in this paragraph are as originally published in 1980.—TRANS.

and international symposia on the issue have accomplished nothing else in the end than to tell us what was already obvious: that television is different from the print media.

In his book Rivers recalls the comments of a citizen asked about this subject during the newspaper strike: "I lack the details but I know the results. It's almost like reading the headlines without getting into the story. I miss the explanations of events." This individual has probably zeroed in on what's really going on. Essentially, the print media and television, along with the other communications media, are not competitive but complementary. They are competitive only in the area of advertising, and that is a fact well worth keeping in mind. But in most other respects, there are areas where television can barely compete with the print media (analysis, background) while other kinds of stories receive great benefit from the immediacy and visual impact of television. A fundamental problem is that ordinarily television journalists have come from the print media, and they try to impose the laws and manias of newspapers on it. There are some unique aspects of televised information that these journalists should keep in mind at all times.

In the first place, there are time limitations, not only for the news space itself but also because of the fact that the viewer watches the news on television at specific times. Second, there are differences in cerebral capacity for the reception and retention of written versus spoken text. And third, one must consider the global conception the viewer has of the television medium.

A fifteen-minute television broadcast can hold no more than about 1,700 words. A newspaper normally has about 20,000. In terms of capacity the newspaper is much more efficient than the broadcast; it is, above all, a more complete informing medium. Those details that the previously cited strike victim mentioned can only be had in the newspaper. Of the famous five W's and an H (who, what, when, where, why and how), it is the *why* that is most clearly and specifically reserved for the print media, which in the future must come to play a more analytical and explanatory role. In this regard the print journalists in some respects tend to take on for themselves the function of the judge. It does not bother me in the least that this word be assimilated in the list of basic qualities for the practice of print journalism. As we have stated, a newspaper is not only witness to social changes but also actor and driving force in them. Purely testimonial journalism, supposedly objective and impartial, does not exist. What does exist is honest journalism of independent vocation, journalism not subject—and fighting not to be subjected—to outside controls or interests different from those of its readers. This kind of journalism does not have to do battle with television, because it is its indispensable complement. Television is actually its best ally: it announces the news that the readers will then go on to corroborate, extend and comprehend in the newspaper.

News broadcasts are made at fixed times, a dictatorship to which a newspaper does not submit its readers. One can also go back in a newspaper and reread, think over and make comments on its contents. One characteristic of the television audience that broadcast journalists seldom recognize is that rarely does the same viewer watch all the major news broadcasts. In the industrialized countries the tendency is to watch only one, which means that the producers of the newscast must be sure that all important news, and only the important news, be given in each broadcast. In Spain it is true that because there is only one television network the high concentration of viewers it has could mean that many of them do watch two or three news programs. But the general trend is against this, and television journalists here should become aware of the experience of the more developed television networks.

It has now been ten years since the president of CBS declared that while it was true that an American's reading time had decreased because of television, the same did not hold for time spent reading the newspaper. "The newspaper reader," he said at a symposium on the issue, "spends the same time reading his newspaper today that he did fifteen years ago: forty-seven minutes for the college graduate and thirty-seven minutes for the non-college reader." He added, "What has suffered most since the arrival of television, has been radio." Despite this optimism, in Spain, increasing population has not led to increased newspaper circulation. Although the statistics are not very reliable, many experts agree that during and even before the time of the Republic[4] the relative circulation figures were much greater than they are today. What we have today is one copy for every ten readers, which puts us on a par with Italy, but it has to be pointed out that the proportion has not changed for at least the last ten or fifteen years. We are at the bottom of the readership ranking in Western Europe. To blame television for this situation appears to me to be an oversimplification.

---

4. 1931 to 1936, or from the time of Alfonso XIII's abdication to the beginning of the Spanish Civil War.—TRANS.

I think that the fault rests rather with the weak reading habits among Spaniards, and with the old regime's disdain for it and for culture and information in general. It is not that the average Spaniard doesn't read newspapers. He simply doesn't read, or else he reads very little. In this sense television can help educate the citizenry.

Television can be of help in many other respects also. We cannot overestimate the technical assistance that electronics can provide in matters of newspaper distribution. The Spanish National Telephone Company has already begun marketing a system through which one will be able to receive at home, in one's television set, a condensed package of the most important information from the newspaper to which one subscribes for a relatively modest fee. At five in the morning a normal cassette can record a series of coded impulses off the telephone through an automatic answering device, which receives the news package sent out from the newspaper's central switchboard. Later, with a simple converter the user can look at the news and even at advertisements the newspaper has sent out in his house. This system has the advantage of not having to rely on any auxiliary cable transmission system, because it uses telephone lines. And users will be able to acquire the basic equipment at a relatively moderate price. In any case it is cheaper than the systems traditionally used by cablevision and those now marketed in the United States, Germany, and Great Britain.

Many are asking what this novelty is, television or newspaper. It is, I believe, simply journalism, the electronic medium adapted to the possibilities of information. The use of computers in document filing systems along with other similar technological advances will provide sufficient means for the survival of the press, and offer new possibilities and methods to serve the reader. The public of the twenty-first century will be progressively more and better informed.

Cognition and Time

We were saying that a little-known aspect of television in its informative tasks concerns the capacity of the human brain to receive images. A study by ANPA, the American Newspaper Publishers Association, asserted with the support of scientific analysis that the written word can program—to use the analogous computer terminology—human intelligence more efficiently than can the spoken word. The same study showed that a normal individual is capable of speaking or hearing about 150 words per minute, while even a slow reader can read at least 250 words per minute. Fast readers can reach 1,000 or even 1,500 words per minute. Hence it is evident that the first temporal limit for televised information is set by man's inherent difficulty in the reception of that information. The newspaper will then continue to assure us that what the television has said is true, that we did not get it wrong when we heard it.

Lastly, as I explained at the beginning of this book, a reader who buys a newspaper does not just buy information but a whole and coherent product, which he wants finished from beginning to end, and one which he will not be able to get from television. With all due respect for the ideas of theoreticians on the high participatory value of television as a "cold" medium, there is no doubt in the mind of any journalist that a special kind of intimate and personal communication is established between a newspaper and its reader, which is absolutely impossible for other media to overcome. Readers frequently speak of *their* newspaper and are conscious of the choice they have at the newsstand. Not that the reader will adopt the ideology or positions the paper represents, but it will happen that a special dialogue between reader and writer comes into being, a relationship of which they themselves are actually unaware. Cynics would call this the miracle of communication. I simply believe this to be the reality of dialogue. Perhaps television does evoke collective emotion or participation better than do the print media, but in my opinion the newspaper more efficiently aids a person in establishing his social identity. Thus newspapers can often become symbols of things other than a certain style of journalism or a certain informational slant. How can one deny that when walking down the street with a copy of *El País, El Imparcial, Interviu, El Caso* or *Hola* under one's arm, a lot more is being said than what is contained in these publications. On the other hand, everyone is condemned to watch the same Spanish television.

Television then cannot be considered a real competitor of the print media in the last analysis, and as I have said, one should not look to the former for the causes of the latter's crisis, with one exception—advertising. TVE consumes practically a third of the advertising revenue in Spain, sets prices in monopolistic fashion, often at levels tantamount to "dumping," to which the print media then have to adjust when setting their prices. This brings about additional problems that will not be examined here; suffice it to say that they run from contributing to national alcoholism to dependence on multinational corporations for consumption. And all of this to the tune of billions of pesetas in losses each year. This is the only area in which I see Spanish television operating against the print media today, with its state oligopolistic practices causing irreparable damage to the sector, and above all, to Spanish readers.

Therefore, when one brings up the war between television and the print media for discussion, I believe it is worth one's while to make certain qualifications and exceptions. In any case, television is set *against* the press in two ways: one, through the advertising problems just described, and two, because at this moment Spanish television, as I see it, is *against* the Spanish people. And in this sense, although newspapers have no reason to be against television generically, it is certainly necessary to be against *this* television.

To follow this line a bit further, I would like to reflect on the present problems of ownership and political control of such a fabulous means of communication, and speculate on the immediate future.

At an early point one runs into the ongoing polemic concerning whether television should be state- or privately controlled. It is a many-sided and relatively sterile issue, because television is in some way dependent on the state just about everywhere. Even in the United States, the most flagrant example of a capitalist economy and respect for private property, television channels are federal concessions. What is really important is not so much whether television is state or private, but rather which systems of social control there are, whatever the ownership status. The problem is to figure out how to free our television from the influence of government and political forces and make it serve the public. The only way here is to enforce the already passed statute. But this enforcement should be carried out with scrupulous respect for the media professionals by parliament, because it is the former and not the MP's who are actually socially responsible—at least they should be—for the quality and content of programs.

Unfortunately, recent experience does not allow us much optimism on this point. It looks frightfully as if we are on the road to an Italian model, which consists not of the disappearance of government censorship but of the multiplication of censors by the number of parties represented in parliament. This is a very real danger, and it responds to that fondest dream of parliamentarians that political and democratic life begin and end with them, whence they would essentially become a new version of Franco's National Movement.[5]

An Italian solution would be enormously frustrating, and moreover it would not in any way solve the urgent problems of quality and interest Spanish television has. It is neither untruthful nor sensationalistic nor yellow journalism to

---

5. At first the term *National Movement* signified Franco's uprising against the Spanish government on July 18, 1936, along with the individuals who had begun to "move" to fight against the "enemy." The term was then incorporated into the legitimizing documents and ideology of the Franco state. The 1958 Law of Fundamental Principles defined the National Movement as the "communion of Spaniards within the fundamental principles." Further crystallization of National Movement symbolism came when Franco created a formal organization bearing its name, presided over by a secretary-general (see passage and note 7 on Adolfo Suárez in chapter 7). Franco modeled this quasi-political organization after the Italian Grand Fascist Council. Since Franco had the advantage of perspective—he knew well the role played by the Italian organization in Mussolini's fall—he took steps throughout his tenure to keep the National Movement weak. He constantly played one of his supporting subfactions off against another, and stripped the Movement organization of executive functions. See Manual Vázquez Montalbán, *Diccionario del franquismo* (Barcelona: Dopesa, 1977), 62–63.—TRANS.

emphasize the corruption, waste, pilferage, and poor quality and productivity of Spanish television. It has tremendous structural problems, not only concerning property but also personnel, financing, and technology, and it needs a strong hand to set things straight. And in view of what went on both before and after the passage of the statute, it is unfortunately necessary to ask oneself if there is still time to do anything, if there may yet be a humane and just political solution to the problem of Spanish television.

Chapter 7

The Press and Elections

The electoral influence of the communications media has
been so analyzed by political sociologists and mass media
scholars that little or nothing in the way of theory can be
added here. Professor Charles Wright lays out the problem
simply: "Underneath these questions," he says, "is the fear
that the individual and the public can be manipulated by
those who have access to the mass media." Later he poses
this question: "Are our opinions, attitudes, and knowledge
perhaps so vulnerable that they can be modified by what we
see on television and read in the newspapers? . . ."[1] The citizen's fears of being fooled are further underscored in the
messages we newspaper editors receive. "You who complain
so much about corporate or government pressure don't seem
to realize that we have to put up with the manipulations of
your writers," they usually say. But if a free society really

---

1. Wright, Charles, *Mass Communication: A Sociological Perspective* (New York:
Random House, 1959), 100.—TRANS.

wants to keep well informed then it will have to learn to entrust the information function to journalists, with the understanding that these journalists too will commit errors and that they are not exempt from corruption or sin, but also accepting that they can possess more data and elements of judgment than the average citizen does, and not necessarily any less honesty. Moreover, an elemental inspection by a reasonably educated person, such as the typical Spaniard, will lead him to select a specific publication in which he can faithfully place his trust. The plurality of sources is therefore fundamental for a free society.

The real question is to determine just how far journalists, through the mass media, can go in influencing the results of political elections. These media do affect the personal opinions of each citizen, although it must be pointed out that not all the media have the same degree of influence over those opinions all the time. It should also be understood that *public opinion,* which Ortega[2] chose to call *reigning opinion,* is not just the sum of individual opinions. And to change public opinion, the key to acquiring influence in any electoral process, more is needed than just a good publicity campaign. Above all, a desire for change must exist in the social collective. If we take the referendum for political reform of 1976 as an example, we observe that the government's campaign achieved its goals because it was a massive and overwhelming campaign that coincided with the desires of the Spanish people: for democracy. At least that is how the

---

2. The philosopher José Ortega y Gasset.—TRANS.

Suárez administration's propaganda had aligned itself. The logic of active abstention as a democratic attitude escaped the average citizen, and it was a mistake by the left parties to propose it.

In the general elections of 1977 both the print and broadcast media played a very special role. Newspapers had been so important in the process of Spanish democratization that it was difficult to imagine them in any other way. During the years immediately prior to the democracy we Spaniards had no other dependable public forum than that offered by a few dailies and magazines, so these publications came under a virtual assault by candidates and public figures on the occasion of the first democratic elections. Furthermore, average readers were not yet used to being critical or analytical of the publications they were being presented, so many of them were only receptive to base sensations.

At that time political parties lacked their own means of expression. The publications they actually had in operation were not yet well established, and they tended to remind one strikingly of political pamphlets or student rags. And in addition, from an objective point of view very few of the Spanish newspapers in existence in 1977 could properly claim to be uncompromised by the traditional right. So during that campaign the left parties lacked dailies that openly favored them while the right benefited from ample press support. This by itself shows how unfounded the fears were of those who spoke of the need to watch the editorial staffs, and not editorial management, because many had complained that the former were so difficult to control. The notion that editorial management cannot manage anything, and that they are at the mercy of the lower editorial ranks is comparable to the idea that editorial staffs are plagued with swarms of dangerous and radical leftists who are poised—as they say in argot—to score as many goals as they can.

It goes without saying that some parties have practiced the technique of infiltration in the recent past. Being forced to work underground tends to promote this type of thing. But an increasing professionalism has made the arrogant militance of a few writers—whatever their ideologies or convictions—disappear in the most recent past.

This fear of too-progressive editorial staffs is not, by the way, new or specific to our country. In *The Effete Conspiracy,* Ben Bagdikian relates the fears of the majority of the editors of North American dailies, almost all of them Republicans, who believe their staffs to be overrun with traitorous Democrats.[3] In my judgment the problem is not the personal political affiliation of individuals who make up an editorial staff, but the specific professionalism of each of them. There are entire books dedicated to the problems of a reporter's personal politics, but no clear delineation has yet been made between personal political compromise and becoming a hired gun, most probably because they are too often one and the same person. In those countries where public opinion is more developed, this kind of conflict is minimal. In others like Portugal or Italy, where the degree of political polarization of the press is enormously high, the pressure from the editorial staffs—even from the pressroom floors—is suf-

---

3. Ben Bagdikian, *The Effete Conspiracy* (Boston: Beacon Press, 1972).—TRANS.

focating. Frederich Engels, in an article entitled "Marx and the New Rhine Gazette," wrote:

> The constitution in effect came down simply to the dictatorship of Marx. A great daily newspaper that has to come out at a fixed time cannot consequently defend its points of view under any other kind of regime.

As I am not a Marxist I cannot recommend that others heed this counsel, and what's more, I don't believe in it. To me, personally, dictatorship seems a bad system for anything, besides being unjust, inefficient, and inhumane. As I am a convinced democrat, I know that democracy and authority are not mutually exclusive. One cannot imagine a modern and independent press where its writers do not have means of access and dialogue, of participation, in the control and orientation of the editorial line of its newspapers. This is not to preach for a soviet of journalists—as I have heard one of our conservative leaders say—but rather to defend the rights of citizens. They should know that their right to be informed does not depend exclusively on an editor with money or on a wealthy publisher, but rather on a professional class that is socially responsible for the quality and independence of that information.

I have to emphasize, moreover, that I put no stock in the complaint, more generally held than one might think, that the staffs of today's Spanish dailies are not under control. Some editors pass the blame on to their staffs so that they won't have to offer explanations for their own decisions or mistakes. Not a few ministers use the excuse in order to be able to openly criticize the editorial line of some newspaper without hurting the feelings of an editor friend. And the majority of the owners believe it to be true because they have a reactionary and possessive concept of newspaper ownership. Here a person owns a newspaper as someone owns a plantation. It must be asserted very strongly that this feudal concept of journalistic property has to be stopped once and for all if we want to construct a modern press. I am not saying that intellectuals aren't sometimes easily bought, but never in history have ideas been material for barter. Owners of newspapers can do many things, but they may not detain reality. And those owners who persist in placing their papers in the service of some extraneous interest will make it so that they don't last long. One does not place a publication in the defense of some partial or special interest with impunity.

As for the party press, I do not deny its necessity and utility. But this phenomenon is more necessary from the point of view of the parties themselves and not of the press. I mean to say that it is not so much a journalistic phenomenon as it is a means of organization and aid for a political party. A party press rarely convinces anyone not already convinced, and rarely will it help to win an election.

What is being debated now, nevertheless, is not whether party papers should exist, but rather what position the great independent press and the local and regional dailies should take on the elections.

I said before and will say again that one of the grave problems that confronts us is that the Spanish daily press, almost in its entirety, is controlled by the right. The furthest that independent newspapers have gone is to say that they will await each party's position before emitting their own options or opinions in each case. But we have to admit that things haven't really worked out that way. The left, which can count on the support of a few magazines and the party press, knows that it can hardly ever expect to have the independent press on its side.

It is difficult to say how important this fact will be for the elections, as it is not known to what extent a newspaper can influence a voter or group of voters in changing their vote. In Spain the generally accepted belief is that one votes for a person more than for a party or a program. Another important fact is that people vote in groups, especially in rural locales. This is to say that people's votes are influenced not so much by the mass media as by the personal opinions of each group's social leader. And the success of a party largely depends on the extent to which it can manage to influence these leaders. The leader in these towns is usually the mayor, the doctor or the priest.

This illustrates—from a sociological and not just a political point of view—the importance the apparatus of the old regime has acquired in the campaigns for democracy. The government has always been able to rely on this system of groups and social leaders to tip the balance in their favor, at least in some parts of the peninsula. In more than a few places it has also been aided by ecclesiastical authority and organization. The Church, together with what remains of the Movement,[4] is the other large power bureaucracy that exists in Spain. It has a very loyal communications network and, contrary to what some people think, it maintains a

---

4. Franco's National Movement organization.—TRANS.

hierarchical structure so firm that it is a campaign instrument of the first rank.

The media organization Edica[5] continues to evoke feelings of fear and reverence among the politically powerful in our country. Its current group of young leaders is tremendously astute and audacious. With bold and adept strokes this aptly nicknamed "holy house" continues to place large numbers of its own in the governments of Suárez.[6] If we consider that many of these ministers and representatives were board members of the same newspaper—one of them is its editor in chief—any speculation on the position of Edica with respect to the elections appears superfluous.

The Movement, or what is left of it, is, as we have pointed out, the other major component of the last few governments. It is important to realize that Suárez *fue cocinero antes que fraile,* and he reached the presidency from the position of General Secretary.[7] Presumably this is an organization he knows inside out. Under the name "State Media of Communication," the Movement maintains a huge chain of

---

5. Editorial Católica, founded in 1911 to ensure a Catholic presence in the public sphere. As Cebrián implies, it has grown in power over the years.—TRANS.

6. Adolfo Suárez was appointed prime minister of Spain in July, 1976, and his UCD center-coalition party won the first parliamentary elections in June, 1977. He was prime minister at the time the Spanish edition of this book was written and resigned in January 1981, succumbing to a long-festering political crisis. A good account of this period is Paul Preston, *The Triumph of Democracy in Spain* (London: Methuen, 1986). The newspaper to which Cebrián refers is probably the Madrid daily *Ya.*—TRANS.

7. Suárez was General Secretary of Franco's National Movement organization. I cannot find an equivalent metaphor for the untranslated phrase, which is literally "Suárez was a cook before he became a priest." The gist of the phrase is something like this: before aligning himself with powerful liberal and conservative Catholic interests, he had tried to make his political fortune through his Falangist and Movement ties.—TRANS.

newspapers—the biggest in Western Europe—which consume hundreds of millions of pesetas a year from the public trough, and which in most instances has not abandoned a line of assistance to the bunker.[8] We Spaniards have a right to demand that something be done about these newspapers before we return to the polls. It is cynical to have them maintained, like the broadcast networks, by a minister or secretary of state. If the press of the Movement served the spirit of its founders it would have to show itself in favor of dictatorship and totalitarianism. But those things are now against the penal code. If it follows the dictates of democracy it will forsake the ideology and positions it has served since its founding. The Movement Press—or State Media of Communication—is not an electorally clean press and it must be transformed as soon as possible. It cannot be said that this is a novel request. Many of us have been making the case publicly for years. Local entities or perhaps some private firms could well take charge of certain of the chain's papers and radio stations. Others will perhaps have to disappear. But in all cases the government should first offer reporters and workers the chance to develop plans for participation and cooperative management or something similar.

The electoral attitudes of the rest of the print media should also be scrutinized. I am talking about the weighty

---

8. The term *bunker* refers first of all to Hitler's fortified command post during the last months of World War II. In this context it refers to those among the political class who are intransigent in their desire to maintain the institutions and ideology of Francoism. Of those names discussed previously in this book, José Antonio Girón de Velasco would be considered a central figure in this disparagingly regarded but still feared group, along with the journalist Emilio Romero.—TRANS.

independent press, slightly or squarely to the right, that we have in this country. The new newspapers among them are quite ardent and less compromised by the past, also more vehement, and too anxious to fix everything once and for all and as soon as possible. They are subject to two major temptations: they either wish to openly or cautiously support some particular political party, or else they try to maintain a neutrality so pure and exquisite that they turn into dull antiseptics for the reader, and end up contributing nothing constructive to the future of the country.

Newspapers in other countries sometimes have the questionable custom of making recommendations and endorsements for an election. When the options are few—two or three—it creates fewer problems, but it can be more compromising when an election is held under more pluralistic conditions. Newspapers have a right to do this, but they should not lose sight of the risks involved. In principle, supporting a specific stance should not harm the independence of a daily, but there is little doubt that in practice, when the witch-hunting begins, its credibility will suffer. As it suffers when one sees its editors, president or editorial writers working in the ranks or at the head of political parties, and leaving their publications—professedly neutral—with an unmistakable and unfortunate partisan stain.

On the other danger extreme, one finds the desire to hold to such a strong neutrality that one ends up saying nothing, therefore adding to the confusion. Not every Spaniard who says he's founded a political party and goes out and gets it officially registered has the right to equal treatment in the pages of the great dailies. He first has to make a solid effort to propose something valid and coherent for this country.

Unfortunately, there are a lot of dreamers and opportunists who run their parties like private ranches, and their sad example shows only that politics is not a game or an adventure, but a service with historic responsibility.

Belligerence in favor of democracy justifies not supporting any specific party, but also not treating all parties alike. The great historical interests and currents of thought are what should always be represented in our parliament, and it is the leaders of these currents, leaders also of the Spanish people, that the great independent dailies should support and to whom they should show partisanship.

If our newspapers learn to collaborate in this way for the construction of democracy, if we do not shy away from polemics but also do not get tangled up in personal interests and absurd campaigns, if we assume the task of encouraging dialogue without meddling in it ourselves, if we learn how to be discriminating yet fair at the same time, to be adversaries but not enemies, friends but not accomplices, then I am convinced that the Spanish press will play a great stabilizing and explanatory role in the next electoral campaigns. If, however, we turn our pages into palaces of intrigue, schools of adoration, closets for skeletons, and fields fertilized with inflammatory rhetoric and accusations, we will contribute to the erosion of the possibilities of coexistence and make it an easy game for those working for the return of the dictatorship.

At one time I said that Spain is at a critical juncture in the construction of a young democracy. Democracy is neither the solution to all problems nor the best of all worlds. It is only the least bad of the systems that people who have to live together possess. And it is important not to disillusion the younger generations, who are tired of authoritarianism and anxious for freedom, for the experiences to which that word gives prospect. Freedom is a word that, despite so much cheapening and manipulation, continues to mean something for which hundreds of thousands of people have fought, often to the death, throughout history.

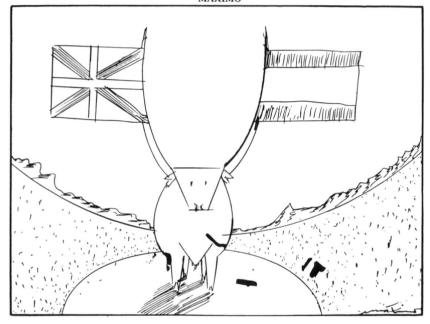

El País

Chapter 8

Freedom of the Press in the Constitution

The assertion that freedom of expression is one of the basic conditions for democracy is so obvious that it hardly warrants theoretical development. It is self-evident that democracy is only possible where there are democratic regimes. Freedom of the press, then, in its history and objectives, is consubstantial with the construction of parliamentary liberalism and modern constitutionalism. During their formation, countries such as the United States were influenced in a major way by the emerging idea of press freedom; they have made freedom of expression one of the fundamental elements of the state. "The basis of our government being the opinion of the people," said President Jefferson, ". . . whether we should have a government without newspapers, or newspapers without a government, I should not hesitate a moment to prefer the latter."

Freedom of expression is certainly a major part of the collective of public rights and freedoms recognized by democratic systems, and its development cannot be attained without parallel development of other democratic institutions. The incapacity of authoritarian or totalitarian regimes to coexist with a system of free press has for Spaniards been demonstrated empirically in the recent past. While it did not embrace the principle of freedom of expression, the Law of the Press of 1966 did at least eliminate prior censorship, and therefore constituted one of the breaches—probably the only one institutionally speaking— through which the opposition to the dictatorship could operate and contribute to the social and political transformation of the country. Thought of as one of the liberalizing steps promoted by some reformists within the Franco regime, the Fraga Law was considered by the regime's more orthodox members to be a veritable torpedo at the water line of the old ship of state. The "noxiousness" of its effects—in their view—provoked the stagnation of other projects of similar revisionist cloth, concerning what was referred to then as political associationism, and also of the right to unionize and to strike. In 1969 the then-vice-president Admiral Carrero Blanco[1] was still justifying the need for a state of emergency throughout the country on account of the social disintegration that had befallen it largely, in his under-

---

1. If one person could have been called Franco's right-hand man during the last years of his rule, it would have been Admiral Luis Carrero Blanco (1903–73). Closely aligned with the Catholic organization Opus Dei, he was appointed vice-president of the government in 1970 and president of the Council of Ministers in 1971. It looked as if he was to become Franco's successor, but that line of speculation ended with Carrero's spectacular assassination at the hand of the Basque separatist group ETA in 1973.—TRANS.

standing, because of the freedom of expression—which at that time did not really exist.

Due to this peculiar situation, the press, subjected to a system of self-censorship but freed from prior censorship, was able to contribute to the expansion of political dialogue and let a little fresh air, so to speak, into the dank, decrepit intellectual and cultural hole the dictatorship had thrown us into. For a long time the voice of society, silenced in the legislature, on television, in the pulpits and in the streets, laboriously began to find itself among the pages of some newspapers and magazines. The experience came to illustrate once more that the press is not limited to witnessing events, but rather acts, through the communication of news and ideas, as a vehicle for social change. If only through building awareness of such events, the press spawned new behaviors and images of reality. It is precisely upon this capacity that the desire to manipulate and control the mass media by power—whatever its manifestation—is based. This goes along with the convention that the first and foremost of man's powers is that of awareness. The electrification of the modern world, the acceleration of transmission speeds and the superabundance and complexity of human relations has pushed the power of this role of information as a vehicle for social mutations to unsuspected limits.

This transforming character of the press was illustrated, as we said, in the last years of Francoism and even more so during the period of transition to democracy. We can now clearly see that issues such as political amnesty and the legalization of the Spanish Communist Party were resolved without grave difficulties thanks in large part to the work of idea diffusion and preparation of public opinion² carried out beforehand by the communication media. Journalists and newspapers collaborated—and not without risk—in the tasks of the political development of our country. And if this is now all history, it is nevertheless well worth remembering when it comes time to analyze where the media question stands today, and what lay on the horizon for the Spanish communications media after the passage of the constitution of 1978.

Freedom of Expression in the Constitution

The right to freedom of expression is recognized in Article 20 of the Spanish Constitution of 1978, which reads textually:

1. The following rights are recognized and protected:
   a) to express and disseminate thoughts, ideas, and opinions in writing, speech, or through any other means of reproduction.
   b) to literary, artistic, scientific and technical production and creation.
   c) to academic freedom.
   d) to freely communicate or receive true information by any media of diffusion. The Law will regulate the conscience clause and professional secrecy with respect to the exercise of these freedoms.

---

2. "Preparation of public opinion" is an approximate translation of *mentalización*, the substantive form of "to mentalize." This would have been understandable if rendered "the mentalization of public opinion," but it would also have been a neologism. Would we like to have such a word in our language?—TRANS.

2. The exercise of these rights cannot be restricted by any type of prior censorship.

3. The law will regulate the organization and parliamentary control of the media of communication dependent on the State or on any public entity and will guarantee access to said media by significant social and political groups, with respect for the social pluralism and diverse languages of Spain.

4. These freedoms are only limited with respect to the rights recognized in this Document, in the precepts of the laws that develop it and especially with respect to the right to honor, to one's privacy, to one's own image, and the need to protect the young.

5. The seizure of publications, recordings, and other means of information may only be carried out by authority of judicial resolution.

Here in legal arguments of questionable worth—but nevertheless clearly asserted—we have the right of all Spaniards to freedom of expression. This is obviously a right of all citizens, the practice of which has historically given rise to both the mass media, which are now themselves institutional in character, and to a professional class of people called journalists. It is appropriate to point out that this institutional character of the press just mentioned has led to its traditional consideration as the "fourth estate." This view, which in our day comes from considering Montesquieu's divisions of power as immutable and time-proven, brings with it a number of corollary notions. Institutionally speaking, the press—and to say "the press" we are thinking of its extension as the communications media in general— certainly possess a high degree of power, but one could say that it is power insofar as it is used to control other powers. It is, from this point of view and in my judgment, rather a countervailing power, a limiter of abuses, and especially the abuses of the executive, which is itself becoming increasingly broad in its actions and propaganda.

In this sense the critical or adversarial function of the press becomes irreplaceable, and it certainly has to be the origin of many and very old conflicts in the exercise of the constitutionally recognized right of freedom of expression.

Although there are many political, legal, and professional aspects of this right that should and could well be analyzed, our discussion here will focus basically on structural problems affecting the communication media in Spain, and especially on those that affect the people who have taken freedom of expression and have made it into a professional duty and a means of living: the journalists.

Spanish journalists today face problems critical to their development as a professional body. There are problems of training and internal organization, of specific preparation with respect to their tasks, and of organization for the defense of their own common interests.

That the Law of the Press of 1966 is still in effect (although with some substantial modifications) means among other things that a statute for journalists exists, which outlines the basic principles of the profession. A common denominator in many Western journalistic circles is the belief that the best Law of the Press is no Law of the Press, and that any document of this kind does nothing more than limit the constitutional right to freedom of expression. Here, nevertheless, in accordance with our legal situation, the practice of the journalistic profession is subject to academic and administrative red tape in the form of the obtaining of a degree in information sciences and the subsequent obtaining of a press card, or what used to be called an official card. The existence of a single means of access to the profession is in contradiction to both the liberal principles that gave life to the freedom of the press, and to the rational argument that the communications media require a broad variety of experts from many different branches of learning. It also goes against reality, as long as there are large numbers of Spaniards who do not have that degree, but who despite this assume the social responsibility—some of them superbly—demanded of the journalistic profession.

The maintenance of a formal restriction such as the single means of access to the profession, far from guaranteeing the proper training of professionals, has contributed to its bureaucratization. The experience of the School of Information Sciences is revealing. Founded for motives and objectives still unclear, its internal structure, plan of course work and even the often arbitrary nature of the selection of faculty, together with the reality of the job market, have turned these colleges into academic factories of journalistic unemployment. This has also led to the emergence of two classes or castes of journalists, or maybe even three—those with a press card and those without, those with the degree and those who came out of the old school of journalism— and these groups have fomented disunity in the profession. Meanwhile these colleges have not yet dealt squarely with the considerable problems of professional training and objectives. Certainly the ones who have suffered most from the experiment have been the students. They are subjected to arbitrary and sterile training divorced from the problems of the professional universe, and are manipulated in the attainment of petty personal ambitions of some of the heroes of patriotic journalism. Society has a right to demand that those who assume the responsibility of informing have sufficient moral and intellectual preparation when they work in the mass media. The proper development of the journalist is essential for the modernization and political development of the country. Knowing how to combine this training with the necessary freedom, to distinguish it from the creation of closed professional bodies or castes, and how to turn journalism into a profession open to all citizens while at the same time guaranteeing a minimum of coherence and social responsibility in those who hold the keys to the communications media, is the great challenge of our time. Such a challenge is absurd, impractical, and dissipating to try to confront through corporative solutions of the kind that exist now and, unfortunately, are on the horizon.

The promise to take a step toward guaranteeing freedom of expression by passing a Law of Information should instead be considered more like a threat than anything else in this area, and in others as we shall soon see. Limiting the practice of journalism through academic requirements contradicts the liberal spirit of the Spanish constitution.

The conscience clause and the right to professional secrecy, both expressly recognized in the constitution, should be analyzed in this same light. The conscience clause is an attempt to provide journalists with a moral lever over the editorial line of their newspapers. It is derived from the idea, which I hold, that the true proprietors of information are the citizens, or the readers in the case of newspapers. Journalists are the administrators of a right of others, and are the ones in whom readers entrust their confidence when they buy or read a newspaper journalists edit. The same argument can be made for the other communication media. This also presupposes that the publishing corporation acquires a responsibility to its readers, those who give meaning to the newspaper, and for this reason the paper cannot be allowed a change in editorial orientation that would betray the confidence deposited in it. Journalists would be the professional conscience of a paper's readers, and a change in its orientation would thus go against the conscience of the journalists, who are not contracted exclusively to make a newspaper in generic form, but rather to work for a specific newspaper, which cannot and should not be qualitatively transformed. The conscience clause has been the source of long and bitter battles in the Western press. The philosophy of the capitalist organization of a firm applied to the mass media means that a simple transfer of stock should allow decisive change in the editorial line of a daily. The final position of journalists is to consider this kind of transaction a unilateral breaking of the work contract by the firm, for which reason insufficient grounds for firing could be claimed by a journalist should he decide to resign.

Journalists aspire to take this individual right of theirs and use it to render changes in a publication's orientation by the simple will of the proprietor impossible, or at least extremely difficult. It follows from the theory, we insist, that the owner of a newspaper does not own the right to information, which the citizens—concretely the readers of that publication—possess.

The observance of the conscience clause leads inexorably

to conflict between the professional collective of a medium and the business firm that owns it. Other ancillary rights are covered in the jurisprudence in this area. But what is essential is the determination that the owners of a communication medium are not the owners of the news they publish. Juridically the subject suffers from so many gaps and ambiguities that it is quite difficult to arrive at a solution. In the last analysis a conscience clause is only possible and imaginable on the basis of a pact between journalists and publishers to determine what kind of a newspaper they want to make. Later this pact would become solidified through the adhesion of its readers, the ultimate moral level on which the conscience clause attempts to operate.

From the practical perspective, this threatens to be highly inoperable. For the determination that there has been a qualitative change in work conditions, a judge must first find that there was indeed a change in the publication's editorial line, a step that itself is fraught with problems not at all difficult to imagine.

Something similar can be said with respect to professional secrecy, about which a lot more literature has been produced, especially on the struggle for it, which has been waged, basically, by journalists in the United States.

The right to professional secrecy can be defined as that which information professionals have to not reveal their sources, not testify before judges on events they cover in their stories, and not to turn over their personal notebooks, magnetic tapes, or any other materials they may have used in gathering their information. In reality this right is primordially—and many thinkers, like Escarpit, explain it this way—the journalist's ethical duty: not to act as a discloser of his sources of information. If one wants this attitude to be legally protected, it is because it is thought that if informing sources are not absolutely certain of the discretion of journalists called to testify, a lot of valuable information, and valuable in the function of the press as a controller of power, would disappear from circulation.

The history of professional secrecy and journalists' struggle for it is now old. It goes back precisely to 1734, the year in which an editor and publisher of a New York weekly spent nine months in jail for refusing to reveal the identity of the authors of an article against the governor of the state. There have been two cases in Spain, both in 1976: two journalists were tried, one of them by a military tribunal, for refusing to identify the participants at secret press conferences by the Democratic Junta and the Democratic Military Union.[3]

The present constitutionalization of the right of secrecy does not resolve any of these problems, in that the relevant paragraph says it is to be regulated by law, so the ulterior limitations to this right are determined by regulations. In my opinion, a simple reform of the law of criminal sentencing, including journalists among those exempt from testifying in the performance of their work, and the application in the same sense of Article 8, Number 11, of the Penal Code would suffice to guarantee professional secrecy for journalists. This article excuses from responsibility "those who work in fulfillment of an obligation in the legitimate exercise of a right, job, or task." The consideration that this is

---

3. Both groups were founded in 1974. The first was a Spanish Communist Party attempt to form a coalition of prodemocratic forces in Paris. The second was a small group of military officers in Barcelona who decided to organize and struggle for a democratic transition.—Trans.

a right—in this case a constitutional one—and also an obligation to protect the secrecy of sources of information, would be enough to prevent journalists from being charged for withholding of evidence or contempt of court if they refuse the demands of judges.

But instead, the specific codification of a right in this fashion leads one to suppose that a set of exceptions to its practice will come to exist, exceptions that will threaten to destroy the right itself. The most common and notable of these is usually the allusion to state security: when it is in danger, journalists should have to testify. But the problem always resides in determining who decides whether the security of the state is in danger, and in how to distinguish the security of the state from that of a particular executive administration. And for those of us who think—following the aforementioned argument of Jefferson—that part of the security of a democratic state is based on the freedom of expression, whatever attempt is made on the latter appears to us to compose a considerable threat to the security of the former. Clearly, this system of regulatory limitations can conflict with the intent legislators had when they chose to have professional secrecy recognized in the constitution. Moreover, it should not be regarded as a privilege. Journalistic secrecy, in the words of the illustrious Professor Rodríguez Mourullo, not only guarantees a particular professional interest, but it is also a freedom

> that constitutes a fundamental right and is the common property of citizens. Without this guarantee of secrecy a large part of those sources that today provide the information which the press diffuses would remain mute, and the result would be a definitive mutilation of the effective right of information.

But as we have said, the actual practice of this right will lead to uncountable difficulties, above all, if journalists understand it to be, as we noted earlier, an ethical obligation that could well land them behind bars on many occasions. In my opinion, the journalist should never, in any case, reveal his sources of information if the latter wish to remain secret, and I hold this even in cases where they are called in to testify before a magistrate, including situations that comprise legal exceptions to the exercise of this right.

These two questions—on the conscience clause and professional secrecy—are not the only ones that pose problems with respect to the development of the freedom of expression recognized in the constitution. The previous allusion to the state communication media gives sufficient motive to comment here on the developments within its two divisions of the print and telecommunications media. The state press has undergone a first treatment with the disappearance of the newspaper *Arriba,* the agency Pyresa, and another eight of the chain's newspapers. The currently denominated "institutional press" is nothing more than the old propaganda apparatus of Francoism, which had created an immense network of local and regional dailies—often on the basis of expropriations from their old owners—with the sole objective of constructing an "agitprop" for the regime. The maintenance of these newspapers after the passing of the dictatorship has cost the state budget billions of pesetas.[4] Many of them have continued with the same editorial management and staffs, who are totally addicted to the ideology and postulates of the old regime. The parties of the

---

4. In 1980 a billion pesetas was worth about $11 million U.S.—TRANS.

left have fought hard for the continuance of this chain, which they believe—in a most gratuitous way—stands apart from the manipulations of capitalist property, and which they perhaps aspire to control or make profitable, something they have been able to do only on a handful of occasions. This attitude has provoked such humiliating spectacles as the historical organ of Spanish fascism defending Marxist or liberal positions without concern for scruple by any of the parties involved.

The question of the state press has served to illustrate the theoretical impoverishment of the Spanish left as far as the communication media are concerned. Any state press ends up as government press. It is not only the financial question—on the massive losses that need to be covered—that calls for an urgent solution to the problems presented by the maintenance of the old Movement press. It is the very philosophy, the political stance, of a new state on the road to consolidation. A state press is incongruous with a constitution of democratic inspiration. It ends up succumbing to the manipulations of political power and, finally, it is turned into its propaganda instrument.

A solution to this problem can be had such that the acquired rights of the workers and professionals, who are not responsible for the contrived situation, are not violated; and also without recurring to an accelerated Malthusian solution for those newspapers, many of which would remain viable under a new ownership structure. In this regard the autonomous communities, local administrations and organizations can often be prime candidates for stock ownership. But even these remedies would be bad if the editorial staffs or newly formed journalist cooperatives expressed a desire to take them over. I will not deny the difficulties these kinds of solutions have met in the past, nor the probability that many of these employee-owned ventures would later want a private firm to take over. But in my judgment the first decision should remain in the hands of their workers, with particular emphasis on those of the journalists, the moral guarantors, as we have come to see, of the information reaching the readers.

Finally, one cannot end this brief discussion without bringing up the world of the airwaves. One can say without fear of equivocation that, in matters of communication since the advent of democracy, if there has been an immobile and impermeable bastion from the process of change that has taken place in our country, it has been television. Not so for radio—one should not forget that radio broadcasting in Spain began in private hands—which under competent administration has noticeably improved in both its service and in public acceptance.

The debate on television—as on radio in other countries—centers principally on the question of ownership of the medium. While it is true that from positions regarding free initiative as one of the pillars of democratic pluralism it is incomprehensible to defend the theory of state monopoly, one has to recognize that radio and television use a public good—the airwaves—which should be submitted to regulation or leasing by the state. This is the way it is in practice even in the most economically liberal countries like the United States. In ours it has been demonstrated that, insofar as radio broadcasting is concerned, a system of mixed ownership has given excellent results, while what has come about for television is there for all to see. But to cast all aspects of the problem of TVE in terms of ownership appears excessive. All over the world there are private television networks that are manipulated by political and financial power, just as there are state television networks the world over that are fine examples of autonomy and freedom to inform. I am not therefore going to enter into the ongoing debate over whether the recently passed statute for RTVE does or does not provide an opening for the privatization of that medium. I sincerely do not believe that this is going to come about in the short run, and moreover I do not believe this should be considered at a time of absolute crisis and impoverishment of the state network. It will be interesting, then, to find out if the complex system of checks and balances provided by the statute will permit increasing autonomy, freedom, and professionalism for television. What happens in the next few months will be very noteworthy in this regard, and any prediction offered now would be really going out on a limb.[5] In addition, the provision of regional television channels to the autonomous communities will be a further test of the viability of competition in this area.

This has been a brief review of the principal problems that face the press and the mass media in general in our country at this time. There are many others that still need to be addressed. Issues such as the future statute for the state news agencies, the questions surrounding unioniza-

---

5. Cebrián speaks of subsequent changes in the status of state television in the Preface to the U.S. Edition. Changes since then will be difficult to follow or predict, since the question of Spanish television is now being affected by both internal political and economic factors and by Spain's integration into the European Economic Community, an entity that is also struggling over the question of public versus private television.—TRANS.

tion and professional organization of journalists, the business problems facing the print media, and pressures that are pushing against freedom; these are all issues that should merit our equal attention. What I wish to say finally is that the solemn constitutional declaration of a right such as the freedom of expression is not enough, as we all know too well, to guarantee the exercise of that right if certain social, political, and legal conditions are not present to make it possible. If I have been able to contribute at least to the sowing of doubt and disquiet concerning the real threats that hover over the free press, I will be satisfied.

SCHOEN, CRANACH, maximo

1535
1545
1983

El País

Chapter 9

Politicians and Journalists

"The press represents the totality of human intelligence—civilization itself."[1] This sentence, written when Balzac was only twenty-one or so, marked the beginning of that great writer's journalistic endeavors. We cite it here because the essay that follows owes its textual life to Balzac, a man who some twenty years later and then a well-known writer would be driven to write a satirical essay entitled *The Parisian Press*. It has become standard fare in anthologies as the prototypical mordantly critical essay on the journalistic profession. *The Parisian Press* is the product of disillusionment-turned-disgust; it is Balzac's revenge against critics who had sadistically maligned his work, a bitter denunciation of an institution corrupted by political machinations, money and complacent stupidity. His own view of the press

---

1. Honoré de Balzac, *Monographie de la Presse Parisienne* (Paris: Aubry, 1943). This chapter was originally published in Juan Luis Cebrián, *Crónicas de mi país*, [Chronicles of My Country] (Madrid: PRISA, 1985).—TRANS.

became so cruel and malignant that Balzac—the self-same author of the words cited at the outset—would be compelled to write in now different words: "If the press did not exist it would be necessary *not* to invent it." But Balzac remained a journalist at heart even as he poured out his invective. Thus his statements are passionate and hard-edged, and the result is a superlative document.

A recent rereading of that little essay by the progenitor of the modern novel gave me the notion to parody, or to attempt to imitate Balzac by constructing a brief description of the contemporary press of Madrid. Among the numerous reasons for such an exercise is that I believe that each passing day makes more evident the need for self-criticism in our profession. In an instant I was seduced by the idea that through the Balzacian model I could assume the role of persecuted persecutor, and I wondered just how well I and my colleagues could do in such an undertaking. I believe it to be of no small importance to ridicule our own absurdities and to strive for the articulation of a critique of the press from within. I would like to shape such a critique in as incisive a fashion as I can, as I am tired of our being put on the defensive against destructive ideas brought from without, and in such a posture losing sight of the fact that only nonideas are destructive, that ideas do not destroy but—in the best sense of the word—corrode, incessantly, the barriers between ourselves and reality. So notwithstanding the passage of time and the change of context, I will attempt to describe a few of the protagonists of the press in Madrid in a corrosive, Balzacian vein.

The capital press presents a numerous and varied set of species of political flora and journalistic fauna for our inspection. Please forgive me if I limit myself almost exclusively to Madrid. In this era of movements for autonomy, this time when even the capital city of the kingdom has its own government, it might seem inappropriate or old-fashioned (or even inadvisable) to reduce a description of political life and the battle of letters to the domain of a self-centered Madrid. But at least as regards common sense—and, I fear, not only common sense—Madrid sets the pace for the rest of Spain.

Let me add one more aside, again with an apology for these mounting digressions. Such is the degree of centralization of our autonomizing state that virtually everyone has come to the same conclusion: that the unfortunate coup attempt of 23-F[2] failed precisely because it failed in Madrid, and if anyone were to repeat such an attempt—something that doesn't seem to be on the immediate horizon—they would have to guarantee success in Madrid. To defend freedom in Madrid has always been to defend it in all of Spain. And I believe that the following caustic reflections on the

2. The abbreviation for the famous coup attempt of February 23, 1981, in which the Spanish parliament and ministers of government were held hostage for eighteen hours by a group of rebellious military officers led by Lt. Col. Antonio Tejero Molina. Many others were involved, including Gen. Milans del Bosch, who put his troops and tanks into the streets throughout the province of Valencia. Both of them received long prison sentences, but the person who was perhaps most heavily involved, Gen. Alfonso Armada Comyn, received only six years, a sentence that astounded both the public and the political class. Armada apparently used his closeness to King Juan Carlos to convince ultraright military leaders that the king would be in favor of an overthrow of the disintegrating centrist government. After the coup began he acted to offer himself as a kind of savior of the public order, perhaps hoping to himself head a benevolent authoritarian government, saving the left from right-wing death squads and the country from the evils of socialism. The plan failed when the king came out quickly, forcefully, and consistently for democracy, ordering the military to return to their barracks and the insurgents to give themselves up.—TRANS.

world of letters should be valid for the country as a whole.

I mentioned before that one could find a lot of different types of characters among the press and those in political office. It would be somewhat artless and naive of me to present a complete classification here, as in all likelihood it would take considerable taxonomic effort to handle such an array of insects.

Let me begin by taking up a principal species, one thought to be destined to perish along with the old regime but which, surprisingly, seems to multiply and gain in vigor under the new republic. I am referring to our political columnists.

One can look both left and right and see political columnists, although most of them are found attempting to reconstruct a political center. Some reactionary newspapers—a label befitting any paper of self-importance, in the last analysis—have decided to make themselves into pillars of their own beliefs, and have chosen an appropriate method to do so: brick by brick. Their political columnists shape their articles into bricks, which are then deftly hurled at those in their way. At those newspapers—*El Alcázar* being the foremost example until the election and ascension of socialism brought forth a herd of imitators and competitors—the political columnists frequently act like political *fifth columnists.* Shaken out of the crevices they populated in the Franco regime and where they lay in hiding during the transition, they now spend their unearned salaries conspiring toward a resurrection of Franco. If we were to employ the literary style of these people, we would say that political columnists offend, incite, libel, and pollute everything they can. That is not to say that what they produce is particularly harmful, as much of their work is rather amusing. So patent is the simplicity of their nonideas that these columnists don't even merit the title of clowns.[3] But there are many newspapers—since that is how we have decided to classify these reactionary pamphlets—that employ this brick-by-brick strategy. Writers of this species are stacked up in them like folders in a file drawer. Since it is impossible to read them all every day, the editor in chief would be wise to collect their efforts together on a table and mix them around like a set of dominoes. Such a practice would demonstrate just how impersonal and interchangeable they and their ideas really are.

The assumption has always been that journalists wrote newspapers for readers to read. Political columnists have dispatched with this lousy and archaic notion. When they started out they thought they should tailor their writing exclusively for the so-called political class, but they have changed and their strategy now seems to be leading them in the direction of a species of "journalism of conscience" for the democratic order. Later on they discovered the advantages of polemics, embarked on a kind of correspondence crusade and began their own internal debates, quoting each other with backs turned to everyone else. It now seems that political columnists write only for other political columnists. With their functional habitat reconstructed, one would think we might be ready for the task of classification and labeling of these commentators individually, but such an exercise would be a retrospective illusion. Today these col-

---

3. See note 4 on *El Alcázar* in chapter 2.—TRANS.

umnists don't even read each other; they are individuals within their own class, and are fast becoming the only readers of their own work.

Now there are political columnists who get up in the morning bent on provoking a government crisis. Actually all journalists, myself included, dream of causing such a crisis at least once in our lives. We like to imagine ourselves as the motive force behind a steady stream of newly constructed Watergates. Political columnists have a special advantage, however. They have a corner of a page daily reserved for themselves alone. Since not even their editors in chief read them, they use their hard-earned freedom to fabricate poison darts. This practice would strike fear throughout the world if people actually paid attention to what they were writing.

Sometimes some people do become aware of what they are saying, usually by way of confidential press summaries, which are glorified collations of standard press clippings. (Strangely, this method does seem to give the articles a gloss of *top secrecy* that somehow flatters politicians and executives and leads them to give more credence to photocopies than to the printed page.)

Having decided to provoke a crisis, the political columnist can expect to receive a phone call from his intended target if that poor soul happens to come across what the columnist wrote. It occasionally happens that no press secretary or clipping service will have noticed and passed along the poison dart in question. No problem. The columnist will simply lay in wait for the minister or government official in the corridors of parliament, corner him there and with a big smile offer apologies "about that thing this morning. Please

Politicians and Journalists

don't take it as a personal attack." Said minister will no
doubt accept the apology, but he will then quickly scurry
away to the reading room to find out why the columnist was
apologizing.
Political columnists spend a lot of time down at parliament. They occasionally use the seats reserved for the press;
they are more likely to be found in their preferred setting
at the parliamentary cocktail lounge. Some political columnists have made a straight trajectory from lounge chair
to a seat in Congress. Until Peces-Barba[4] closed it down,
politicians used to hang around the lounge between sessions
or when the opposition was delivering its boring speeches.
There they would wait until the bell sounded reminding
them it was time to vote. While in the lounge politicians
would exchange views with journalists and invite them out
to dinner and drinks at taxpayers' expense. It should be
pointed out that not all journalists found down at the lounge
were of the political species. There were also television and
radio reporters along with some other kinds of professionals
who didn't quite qualify for free perks from political
dignitaries.
There were a number of political columnists who would
spend their time at the lounge picking up women, or at least
trying to, or else plotting revenge against the object of a
failed attempt. "If you want, I can make you famous, baby,"
they would whisper to a young communication student who
had come down to the bar to drink from some fountain of

---

4. Gregorio Peces-Barba is a Spanish Socialist Workers Party politician and former president of parliament. He was also a key writer of the 1978 Spanish Constitution.—TRANS.

knowledge within reasonably easy reach. Later she would find herself cited somewhere in small black letters, perhaps even before the evening of eternal gymnastics but certainly after.

While dining at expensive restaurants political columnists are usually found convincing ministers of the transcendent status of the institution of the fourth estate. Quite a few ministers are convinced before they hear the arguments and get right to the task of buying themselves a columnist or two. If market conditions are tight, they'll aim for ad hoc leasing arrangements. Despite President Suárez's efforts to consolidate his slush fund activities under the expert management of a single fakir—the inimitable Mr. Meliá[5]—neither the constraints of tradition nor financial audits have been able to keep slush funds and personnel from coming in over budget. Slush columnists—though clearly not all columnists are of this subspecies—have the shortest of direct lines to the politician who has managed to corral them for a few grand a month. The politician asks not for favors for himself, but for assistance in the task of national salvation. In this way neither slusher nor slushee need feel any remorse. Politicians aren't the only ones using this method. Bankers, executives, and pressure groups often compete in the subtle task of buying journalists. "It's cheaper than buying newspapers," they assure us.

Some people can afford to have a stable of columnists at their call morning, noon, and cocktail hour. The stable

---

5. Josep Meliá, government spokesman under Adolfo Suárez, was a member of the inner circle of advisors to Suárez, which was called the *fontaneros,* or "plumbers."—TRANS.

changes with the solar seasons. The most highly sought journalists are the most flexible, those who can make themselves useful in a pinch as circumstances demand with a rumor here, some gossip or small talk there, maybe a little waffling, something for when the going gets hot or for cooler times—the demand is highest for those who can do whatever it takes to earn their slush.

It goes without saying that not all daily columnists are politicians or corrupt or idiots or wretches. Francisco Umbral is one of the notable exceptions in this sea of mediocrity. I am not standing up for Umbral here because he wrote for *El País,* the fact is that he wrote for *El País* among other reasons because of my sympathy for and solidarity with him. Umbral is the quintessential anticolumnist; his writing is so good that even its flaws deserve to be recorded.[6] I would not hesitate to rate Umbral as the Spanish Balzac of our time. If he doesn't push himself to write a new *comedie humaine* then he will only be the Larra of the twentieth century. For every Umbral in the Spanish press there are dozens of old-guard columnists who wield their pens like dull axes, and other dozens of neodemocrats whose writings render patently false the old dictum that to write in Spain is to weep, for through their work we see that it is no longer the writer who has to weep, but the readers.

Let's leave the political columnist for a moment and fix our spotlight on the figure of the politician-as-columnist. This is a quite colorful species and one about which I have written on other occasions. Politicians-as-columnists try to

---

6. Francisco Umbral is a novelist and writer who wrote a daily column entitled *Spleen de Madrid.*—TRANS.

use newspapers to give speeches they were not allowed to deliver in Congress. They are rarely asked to write an article, yet their offerings fill the copy desks to overflow. They have managed to turn quite a number of managing and chief editors into neurotics. The typical story begins with a politician who writes his copy and sends it off to his targeted newspaper in an envelope stamped "urgent." The next morning the paper's editor in chief is told by his secretary, "Congressman so-and-so is on the line." Newspaper editors in chief in Madrid very rarely accept phone calls, but come the third call from Congressman so-and-so and something begins to make our chief editor suspect that this particular call may be interesting. Maybe there's a little travel involved, perhaps a conference in Santander or Valladolid, maybe even a spot on the party's slate of candidates for Soria.

In their daydreams at the very least, the majority of our chief editors consider themselves congressmen *honoris causa* for a number of districts simultaneously. The politician-as-journalist now on the phone explains to the chief editor the purpose and significance of the article, and the chief editor for his own part says, yes he has read it, though he most certainly will not have done so. At some point in the conversation the chief editor will add that the article will be published—that it is obviously an excellent piece— and will give a concrete publication date for some time within the next two weeks. The chief editor has now managed to gain for himself a fortnight's respite from Congressman so-and-so's phone calls. As this arranged space of tranquility draws to a close, Congressman so-and-so feverishly buys and pores through all the editions of the paper to see just when and where the undelivered speech will shine forth from the printed page. About a day after the promised time period elapses, Congressman so-and-so begins to realize to his horror that the article will not be published. He angrily grabs the telephone and calls the day-dreaming chief editor while trying to hide his irritation: "It's not a question of personal indignation. . . . I'm just trying to find out the reason for the delay in its publication." The chief editor, now convinced that no place on an electoral slate hangs in the balance, puts back in place the formal barriers between the congressman and his person, and will continue to dialogue only through his secretary. His response to Congressman so-and-so will always come from a set stock of possibilities, all meaning the same thing: "It will be out soon," "It's passed out of date," "It won't be published because it's too long." The last excuse is no problem for the congressman. He's always willing to adjust it in any fashion and cut it in half if necessary. Out of date? He'll update it right away.

If the message is simply that the article will not be published, the congressman will set a large and complex operation into motion to get a copy of it back on the director's desk again, just in case the first one was lost or the chief editor hadn't noticed the passage about such and such in his first reading. The paper's chief executive officer, the editor in chief, the political page editor, and the paper's political columnists all receive their very own copies of the non-speech-turned-article, which has now blossomed into a limited edition publication in its own right. The party spokesperson—the one who has the paper's political columnist in his pocket—now intercedes on behalf of the article and the chief editor begins to feel himself enmeshed in a web of pressures and power plays. At this point two things can happen. The speech-turned-article either gets into print or it doesn't. If it does, barely twenty-four hours will have passed its felicitous rebirth as an article before another of the politician's little creatures hits the chief editor's desk, and now no one will be able to convince the politician that it's not Nobel material or even a sacred text.

If the non-speech is not published, a litany of explanations must follow and the author will register his subtle protestations, generally to the effect that—as he will put it—it didn't really matter to him that the article wasn't published, but that he wasn't told earlier that it wouldn't be, so that he could have sent it off to another publication and then . . . . Whatever the course of the explanations offered in any particular instance, a new mental ejaculation by the politician-turned-columnist will inevitably follow, rekindling the process of pushing and prodding to see whether another non-speech will get published in the paper.

A large part of the chief editor's time is spent in petty machinations with these amateurs posing as writers. When a politician-turned-columnist manages to win over an editor in chief, or buy him off or—on rare occasions—when he actually possesses the talent and professional credentials, he becomes a regular feature of the paper. Since there obviously is journalistic talent among the politicians in Spanish parliament, one wonders if we might not be able to work out a system where they could trade places on a regular basis with some of our political columnists, so desirous as the latter are to set the country straight, and so full of . . . formulas to do so.

Outside the time chief editors spend fending off weighty suggestions to print something, they can be found harassed by, reacting to, and otherwise taken to task by someone for something that was actually published. When a current cabinet minister grabs a phone to register his indignation and give a lecture on his version of the concept of responsible journalism to the editor in chief, the latter will never have actually read the offending article, though he will always say he has so as not to give the impression that he doesn't read his own paper. Besides, all that constant reading leaves the chief editor little time for phone conversation, and even with his constant vigilance an occasional piece gets published that he himself did not quite get the chance to fully review. Since in fact in such cases the chief editor hasn't the faintest idea what the article was about, the phone conversation with the minister usually evolves into a most Pinteresque exchange of ambiguities, full of abstruse and at times incredible statements. Once the phone is placed back on the receiver, the editor in chief will call in his senior editor and give him a dressing down in loud and imperious tones for the irresponsible transgression of publishing that article without his approval. Chastened and contrite, the senior editor removes himself from the chief editor's office ready to do penance.

Editors in chief believe that one of their fundamental duties is to dine with important people and be seen at their social events. Some go jealously guarded by security guards to protect themselves from assassination attempts. As the number and quality of one's coterie of bodyguards is a symbol of one's social status, conflicts have begun to arise between certain chief editors and their paper's owners, since the latter do not always see fit to move in public circles with such large escorts themselves.

The responsibilities and demands of his position are a constantly felt burden to the editor in chief. Up early every morning, he might often be observed gazing into his bathroom mirror and uttering an anguished something like, "I have a Spain-ache" to his reflection. *Primus inter pares* in a profession of priests, he thinks of himself as something of a pope of his newspaper, thinking also maybe that he might go out some time and do a little healing of the sick so as to give evidence once and for all of his supernatural ability to deal with reality. Rumor has it that a certain editor in chief has been beatified.

Although editors in chief are quite different from one another, they all share the occupation that—personal and ideological differences apart—makes them resemble each other, kind of as one chicken egg will look like another. They all will insist that they are not irreplaceable, that their paper can survive without them, and that their editorial staffs work smoothly together as a team. Still, when they think of that day when they might be fired, they all dream of the apocalyptic nightmares that would surely result.

Editors in chief are addressed as "Chief" by the editorial staff, just as Franco's cabinet members were called "Minister." I believe this is a throwback to the days of fascist comaraderie imposed during our forty years of peace. An editor in chief—especially one at the helm of an influential daily—is one of the most hated, feared, worshiped, and attacked beings one could imagine. If a chief editor really believed all the good things said about him he would assume the historical role of savior of the kingdom of Spain and her territories—with conviction. Who knows what heights he might reach then—perhaps the directorship of the Spanish wire service Efe or even *El País*.

The pride and hollow arrogance of the editor in chief rubs off on the editorial staff. A kind of Japanese system of charismatic leadership often develops, and this in turn has often led to some strange organizational environments. Many reporters, for example, see themselves as grantors of pardons for the lives of their interlocutors in interviews or fact-gathering transactions. A writer who suffers from the same transcendental mission syndrome that afflicts the chief editor shows potential as a future political columnist.

From a broader perspective the Madrid press operates within a network of small and large conspiracies. Obsessed with themselves and their power, journalists and newspaper impresarios don't merely think of themselves as the backbone of society, they also consider their musings *the* articulations of social reality. Poor readers are thus punished daily with the quarrels one newspaper picks with another. Notwithstanding the return of press freedom, this practice points to an obvious area of underdevelopment in the Spanish press that has yet to be overcome. Contrary to the beliefs of many of our most enthusiastic and ferocious polemicists, this kind of bickering does not increase circulation but diminishes it. Nevertheless we have recently witnessed a new and improved version of the phenomenon. I refer to the reflex action—which is gaining more adherents from those in public administration—of intervening in the pages of newspapers to dissent from or clarify their previously reported positions. The public still remembers the case of the honorable minister of public health who tried to deny through the letters column that he had called the mass poisoning tragedy a simple bug infestation.[7] Not wanting to be left out of the running in this new practice, the Socialist minister of the interior fills chief editors' desks with his letters. The spectacle of a government responding to journalistic criticism by saying "See, I'm not as dumb as you look" instead of explaining the reasons for its reported opinions and statements is extremely insulting to those who believe in representative government. At least there is some consolation for the editor in chief when he can open his mail and see that a certain politician has not yet charmed or corrupted one of his paper's writers—not one of sufficient importance at any rate.

Newspaper polemics are at the same time ephemeral and everlasting. Questions of regional autonomy, television policy, professional issues (such as the licensing of journalists), deserve and receive a lot of space. Let me develop the first of these questions. Although the example comes to mind on the spur of the moment it will suffice to illustrate two chronic flaws of the daily press, flaws that account for much of the success and the decadence of the institution. The first flaw resides in the press's capacity to stir up nationalistic, chauvinistic, patriotic and localistic sentiments among the

---

7. In 1981 almost one hundred people had died from something called "atypical pneumonia" while thousands of others remained horribly ill in hospitals. The minister, Jesús Sanchez Rof, said that it was probably some bug. It later turned out that some distributors had taken rapeseed oil, adulterated it with oil byproducts to give it the color of olive oil, and sold it to the public. The mass poisoning that resulted killed hundreds of people through 1982, further discredited the already troubled centrist government, and exposed the terrible state of institutional protection for consumers in Spain.—TRANS.

people. I have continually maintained a position against nationalism as an ideology, for at bottom it is nothing more than a recent invention that has given to humankind two world wars and millions of deaths. Nationalistic sentiments flare up in all four corners of our country, and in a particularly oppressive Spanish form. In Andalusia we have witnessed the rejection of a director of the 1992 Seville International exposition because he was Catalonian, while in Catalonia a commotion arose over the Pujol litigation, which was allegedly an anti-Catalonian action.[8] Pujol's party Convergència i Unió conjured up some populist appeals with the help of the mass media and performed some short-sighted political manipulations that add up to one of the purest instances of irremediable victimization of the public that can be found in the historical record.

Any victimization suggests the idea of a victimizer, and polemic can thus turn into aggression. Imagine the state of public confusion when spokespersons for Fraga's Madrid faction egged on Catalonian nationalist street demonstrations in Barcelona. Evidently—at least among some of the sterner souls—hatred of socialism (which in most instances turns out to be a kind of game) can lead as far as a renunciation of the concept of the sacred unity of Spain. Upon reflection, maybe there's something to the phenomenon after all.

---

8. Jordi Pujol is president of the autonomous government of the region of Catalonia and Pujol tried to make the investigation of his activities look like a Madrid-based attack on Catalonian nationalism. It should be mentioned that the flip side of regional nationalist sentiments is a common and long-standing irritation over the centralization of political and economic authority in Madrid. The incident involved a very large bankruptcy.—TRANS.

Let's stay with the Pujol example a while longer, since it also brought to the fore the second vice to which I alluded and which is not exclusive to the mass media: envy. When a paper publishes some new story other newspapers commonly question its sources rather than its content. According to these other papers the sources are inevitably confidential or politically motivated *leaks*. This is an extremely ignorant attitude that only brings harm to newspaper readers. All newspapers *lift* stories from other papers, as they say in the professional slang, but the tendency toward nationalistic/chauvinistic competition turns editorial staffs into editorial states ready to do battle with each other with whatever available means. If the resources some papers use to discover others' sources were instead put to work to get their own information, maybe they could be the ones writing some of those same articles. The assumption that all the important news anyone publishes comes from leaks is absurd. Sadly, it seems that we journalists are playing the fool here while our readers—far more intelligently than we—remain more interested in the news than in its sources.

Through the Pujol controversy where established power set up its final line of defense we can begin to make out the contours of certain institutionalizing tendencies—the acquisition of and complicity with power—developing within the Spanish press and its journalists. This process stands out in bolder relief in the case of military reporting. Even today Spanish journalists approach them with the same sacrosanct fear and veneration they have been given for the last five hundred years. The fear stems from the knowledge that one is free, but only conditionally so. As long as the institution of the military remains immune from criticism—as the unarmed are not—this country will not be able to call itself civilized.

The anecdotes and events surrounding the trials of those involved in the 23-F coup attempt brought this point out clearly. The failed coup gave rise to strong expectations that we would be able to engage in serious and civil debate on Army affairs in the pages of our newspapers. I saw only fear and accusations of anti-Spanish motives raised against any who voiced doubt about some of the official verities maintained by those in uniform.

So far as television is concerned I shall add little more to what I have already said. I suppose that since a print journalist has been able to perform this little exercise in honest criticism of newspapers, it should also be possible to extend the method to Spanish Television. Antonio Gala,[9] in a splendid article on the "new journalism" from his well-recognized perspective as master of the Spanish language, labeled the phenomenon "bullshit." I do not happen to agree with this opinion, but since the time of that utterance Spanish Television critics should know that the term may now be used without social or intellectual repercussions.

In the last analysis this has been just an exercise, a little burlesque with a little reflection, by a journalist who believes that the first rule of criticism is self-criticism, and who also believes that freedom of the press is not a sacred phrase but something belonging in the marvelous and indestructible realm of the human condition itself.

If someone has derived some small benefit from this exercise, then the effort was well worth it.

---

9. Antonio Gala is a playwright and for many years a columnist for *El País*. —TRANS.

El País

Chapter 10

Across the Water

In the early 1970s Lord Thompson of Fleet Street, owner of one of the largest newspaper empires in history—that is, until history gave us the gift of Rupert Murdoch—came to Madrid for a short visit. Signs of change were already apparent in the Spanish capital and it was becoming increasingly clear that the Franco regime was moribund. In such an atmosphere the presence of a legendary media figure constituted a major event for the boys of the fourth estate. That faithful subject of the British Crown, a living example of the practical greatness of the Commonwealth, received Spanish editors and journalists in his suite at the luxurious Hotel Ritz. The press professionals streamed into their interviews like a procession of the faithful coming to hear the doctrine of their master. I myself was one of those who made the pilgrimage. Devotedly, I attended the twenty-minute interview that His Excellency had been so kind as to grant my company president, Victor de la Serna.[1] At that time we Spaniards were working hard to overcome the censorship of the Franco regime. We were among the many journalists who were making a serious effort to come up with respectable news under miserable professional, political, technical, and administrative conditions. And in effect the press would play a central role in the erosion of the dictatorship, years later (correctly) proclaiming itself a key protagonist in the process of democratic transition. One can imagine how enthusiastic we were, then, as we approached our interview with this magnate of the printed word who had just recently completed a highly visible takeover of the *Times* of London. We were looking for spiritual and moral support to continue our epic struggle. At the hotel, on a sofa in a rather dark room, sat a corpulent figure whose features could hardly be distinguished for the light but left the effect of a Buddha. The great high priest of the kingdom of the Linotype proceeded to impart his doctrine to us:

"Don't make your newspapers without advertisements."

I won't say that this hit me as a revelation or that it caught me completely by surprise, but I would be lying if I didn't confess my internal astonishment and disenchantment that such an utterance could represent in sum, so simply and straightforwardly, the experience of decades crystallized in the single thought of someone who had dedicated his life's work to the profession that I had chosen.

---

1. A journalist who is son and father of journalists—a member of one of the most famous and respected press clans in Spain.—TRANS.

This was for me a practical lesson that other motivations were to be found in the press across the water, motivations that had not quite made their presence so plainly felt to European journalists, especially to those of us who practiced the craft on the southern flank where this lord of the ink had not yet planted any of his empire's capital. This was the first time that I had come face to face with a genuine representation of a type of journalism that I didn't really know well until then: a kind of journalism that is understood to be above and beyond all other things a business.

Commercialism as a fundamental characteristic of a journalistic environment has long distinguished the U.S. press—and a number of British papers—and continues to do so. While the commercial and marketing concerns of the newspaper business do get taken into account in other latitudes, the Latin mind tends to suspect that the intellectual position of the press, its role as an agent of social change and as a marketplace of ideas, is far more respectable than and superior to any of its other purposes so that one should not, so to speak, profane the corridors of the temple with a plague of merchants. Advertising in the Latin view is a necessary means of survival for the institution of the newspaper and is a facilitator of market exchange; it is generally seen as something marginal to the overall conception of the product. Furthermore, events in Spain in the 1970s led to an exaggeration of this view, mainly because of the peculiar political circumstances I have described elsewhere in these essays. The Latin position embodies a disdainful attitude toward the marketplace and toward aspects of industrial culture in general, and this attitude is shared by most of our country's intellectuals.

This should explain in part my own surprise and indignation at Lord Thompson's remark, which I took at the time to be either too simplistic, too vulgar, or mistaken. In any case it helped me realize two things. First, a newspaper could never be independent if it were not financially so—which is impossible without advertising. Secondly, advertising itself could not be left in the hands of the marketing department while editors washed their own hands of responsibility for the content.

The sometimes disproportionate role that advertising plays for most U.S. papers is striking to those who practice their journalism in the Spanish marketplace.

There are some newspapers like the *New York Times* which for the last decade or so have owed their editorial stability and even their credibility more to their use as an effective advertising vehicle than to their political or intellectual influence. Whether in Italy, Greece, Portugal, or Spain, newspapers often respond first to political or ideological interests, and then allow the squalid state of their self-generated finances to be compensated with generous subsidies from whomever is occupying a seat of power. In such a system it is understood that newspapers are a bad business, which implies the existence of businesses of another genre. Such a system's central principle is this: if you want to impose your point of view on the press, then the press is going to make you pay for the privilege. Marcel Dassault, engineer and creator of one of France's most important industrial complexes, discovered one day that his true calling was to be editor of a high quality women's magazine. *Marie Claire* was the result of this caprice. Similarly, Spanish newspapers have often found themselves responding to the extravagant fancies of one or another kind of visionary. But more frequently, and more importantly, the European press has tended to stare at its own little navel as if it were the center of the universe, secure in the knowledge that theirs was a role so lofty and important that someone would be there to pay for its survival if advertising would not.

In our country the problem of financial environment was exacerbated by the small size of the advertising market, which continues to be extraordinarily small in comparison with the U.S. market. Because of the incredible size of the U.S. market, newspapers there have often become machines for printing money rather than producers of ideas or disseminators of news. For spirits so foreign to Calvinism such as the Spanish this is a mortal sin for which one must not only do penance but also keep from view when committing it.

It seems then that the unjustified scorn with which editorial staffs here look at newspaper marketing departments is compensated for in the United States by the absolutely excessive adoration newspaper owners give to advertising and its related gods. At this stage in my own professional life I can say that Lord Thompson's statement no longer shocks me at all. I believe it effectively true that to publish a daily paper without advertising would be a great mistake, not only because it would lead to a rapid loss of the paper's financial independence—or of the paper itself—but also because advertising now gives readers valuable information, and forms part of the constituting environment of the press and of society as we understand these entities today.

Still, to turn newspapers into mere support structures or vehicles for advertising is a danger from which one should flee like the plague. A newspaper has missions too interesting to allow itself to metamorphose into a suburban shopper or a collection of classified ads. If we grant that a newspaper's independence should rest upon economic solvency, we should then also see that abuse of power in the advertising market will lead to a loss of this independence. Throughout my professional career I have been at pains to strike a reasonable balance in the administration of the following policy: to guarantee and respect my newspaper as a vehicle for advertising, but without making it a slave to advertising. The only slavery that journalists should accept is for the respect of their readers. Paradoxically, the will to serve them will maintain healthy circulation, a fact that will in turn heavily influence advertisers when it comes time for them to decide where to place their ads.

The Myth of Watergate

Watergate and its aftermath continue to form the dominant image conveyed to Spanish journalists by their U.S. colleagues. The influence that this one case has had on the dreams and motivations of journalists the world over has not often been good. While it has naturally promoted investigative journalism and teamwork, at the same time it has promoted hero-worship and created an artificially tense environment for editorial staffs, encouraging them to focus exclusively on scandals of government-toppling potential. This negative consequence of Watergate has made it that much easier for manipulators to influence journalists, something which seems to be manifesting itself through the increasing use of interested and unjustified news leaks. Investigative reporting is all too often misunderstood by young journalists, who keep little statues of Woodward and Bernstein on their altars of hero-gods. This post-Watergate compulsion to seek out the strange or the scandalous has often led to the invention of news stories or to something even worse—their exaggeration.

Personality cultivation[2] is another troubling issue. *Time* magazine, one of the most respected U.S. publications, carefully tries to limit the personal protagonism of its writers, but one can hardly conclude that this is characteristic of U.S. journalism as a whole. When all the debates subside, the popularity of Walter Cronkite remains as crowning testament to the contrary position. If television reporters are normally jealous of the political power and influence over intellectual elites ordinarily wielded by print journalists, the latter often miss not being recognized on airplanes and in restaurants, a kind of public recognition in which television reporters bask. The Spanish press tends to carefully cultivate its own class of idols and this is one of the most obvious among its own set of evils. However, the transformation of the communication process into a show usually helps neither the accuracy nor the credibility of the news. The chief characteristic of U.S. journalism is its tendency to dramatize the news. Its great expressive power resides in the ease in which it proceeds along this course, at the service of an almost uncontested competitive force.

The image one has in Spain of the North American press is, in addition, too closely tied to the quality daily and weekly publications located on the East Coast. What

---

2. Cebrián uses the term *divismo*, which literally means "idolatry."—Trans.

impresses Spanish observers most about the U.S. press are its great liberal tradition, its respect for and defense of freedom of expression, its concept of service to its citizenry, and its pretensions to an appearance of noncommitment to any specific ideology. Far less known to Spaniards are the profiles of those thousands of local and regional papers spread across the United States. These newspapers are sometimes anchored in an ideological provincialism that is convinced that the world ends at the U.S. coasts, and they are published without any consistent intellectual or cultural impulse that could identify their character. But it is not only the small papers that fall into the vice of localism: a general isolationist tendency shared by Americans continues to reinforce their belief that no other universe exists, indeed, which often keeps them from coming to know any other reality than that which they desire to exist.

The victory of marketing wizardry, the proliferation of large firms owning chains of dozens of newspapers, the internal unification of style and content among them, and the use of syndicated columnists are things that have hurt local and regional U.S. publications. Often columnists who appear on their pages are mythic beasts to their readers. They will rarely ever run into one at a cinema house, theater, or bar. The possibility that European readers have of touching, of physically sharing the presence of the most famous journalists, is an additional form of participation with newspapers available to them.

One of the most suspect myths of the U.S. press is its quest for objectivity. By means of a series of norms established to govern the practice of story investigation and presentation to readers, an attempt is made to defend the conclusion that newspapers should be effectively objective if they want to maintain their independence. I have always been skeptical of such pronouncements. No matter how hard journalists try to appear objective, at the very moment they begin to deal with information they assume a quite subjective position. Subjectivity begins with the decision of whether or not to publish a story, and proceeds through decisions on its play—its size, number of columns, location on the page and in the paper. All these decisions imply a subjective element at the moment selection takes place, based on the value judgments of journalists or of those who manage journalists. This is why I have frequently insisted that before being objective newspapers should be honest. They should identify the sources and origins of all their stories—except in those instances where the source must remain secret, and even then some frame must be given to allow the reader to reach understanding. Newspapers must give voice to all parties in a conflict; they should deny neither voice nor platform to any protagonist involved in a story. They should respect human actions and events and not pepper their reports with personal opinions raised in their stead. These are all, in short, more norms of professional honesty than of objectivity.

One of the more oft-diffused lessons of the U.S. press is that fact be strictly differentiated from opinion. Spanish newspapers—not to mention those in France—frequently adopt the custom of commenting upon events before giving an account of them. The U.S. practice of structural separation between the opinion pages and the rest of the newspaper is not well understood in Spanish editorial practice. The figure of the *publisher* as conceived in the United States does not exist as such in Spain. Whether owned by a firm or a family, the content of a newspaper is the complete responsibility of its editor in chief, who attempts to unify the paper's editorial prerogatives with practices more properly identified as generic to newsgathering.

Just what the separation of fact from opinion means is not always clear, especially when one looks at the forms used in interpretive journalism. As the electronic and visual media emerged, print journalism found itself moving progressively toward the practice of explaining rather than merely transmitting the news. It is rather difficult to distinguish between an analysis and a purely ideological alignment of events, between an explanation based on actual events and an opinion ultimately born of individual interpretation. In such circumstances, the challenge to objectivity becomes telling, and in turn makes the need for honesty and transparency in a newspaper's news functions more compelling. It becomes essential to know and report who is doing the talking, when and why they are doing so.

Given all of this, experience teaches that journalists from one country usually resemble journalists from another like so many peas in a pod, the sole exception to this being perhaps Soviet journalists (but in no way categorically including all journalists who work under the various ideological strains of totalitarianism). No longer do the stereotypical renditions of U.S. journalists that early Hollywood films saw fit to disseminate abroad adequately capture the myths and realities of the profession. Journalists in both the United States and Europe share similar concerns and tendencies. Some points of convergence worth pointing out are: the growing number of women on editorial staffs, the enlargement and bureaucratization of the editorial environment and the consequent loss of identity suffered by journalists, the zest with which many journalists take on activist social roles, and the temptations that many journalists face when they begin to include themselves as members of the power elite. Through my readings of books and stories about U.S. journalism and a good measure of personal contact with that culture, I have come to realize that our preoccupations and challenges, what we feel threatened by and what we understand our risks to be, are the same. Even our pleasures, which are not so small as some would imagine nor as scandalous as others would believe, are essentially the same.

The practice of journalism in the United States is both rooted in the best of its historic democratic traditions and a functional part of the contemporary system. Its continual battles against political power, its promotion of public opinion to sacred status, the totality of its forms of operation in effect convert the institution into a part of the overall apparatus it believes it is contesting. There is a contradiction here, which is perhaps inherent to mass media systems in general but which in the United States appears with offensive intensity. Newspapers are an effective counter to economic or political interests, yet even as they perform their contesting functions they form part of the closed universe constituted by those interests.

In spite of all this, U.S. journalists maintain an air of innocence with respect to the reality they describe that it would be inaccurate to call insincere. I suppose this may be a contemporary manifestation of the consistent interest middle-class America has had to both learn and to frame that learning in a studied naiveté. Mark Twain once called reporters troubadours for hire. However, the little ballads they sing are not always music to the ears of social princes. Thus it is not always easy to maintain that initial candor that puts the U.S. press on the side of the facts, however unpleasant they may be. And this is what professional journalists in Spain most admire about our colleagues across the straits: their tenacious and permanent struggle to maintain freedom of expression.

Index